T0197002

This *Side* of *Forty*

# This *Side* of *Forty*

*Exploring the Dynamics of Pursuing
Life's Passions at Any Age*

CATHY GLEN

THIS SIDE OF FORTY
EXPLORING THE DYNAMICS OF PURSUING
LIFE'S PASSIONS AT ANY AGE

iUniverse books may be ordered through booksellers or by contacting:

iUniverse
1663 Liberty Drive
Bloomington, IN 47403
www.iuniverse.com
1-800-Authors (1-800-288-4677)

ISBN: 978-1-5320-4736-7 (sc)
ISBN: 978-1-5320-4735-0 (e)

Library of Congress Control Number: 2018907955

Print information available on the last page.

iUniverse rev. date: 11/28/2018

*T*his book informs and encourages readers to follow their life's passions without allowing one's age to be a deterrent. Are you 40 and younger but have not been enjoying life's journey? The following pages will offer a fresh perspective. The 40 and older group may especially feel inadequate about change. Many feel it's too late to switch careers or start a new adventure; yet they float through life stagnated and inwardly wonder, "what if" they had dared to pursue their dreams. *This Side of Forty* pushes the envelope as it shares true events as well as informs readers, over and under 40, that it's never too late to pursue one's passions at any age!

**by Cathy Glen**

# Contents

## PART 3: LIVE LIFE TO THE FULL!

# Preface

This is a book of encouragement. This book also encourages its readers to stop using "age," whatever yours may be, as a deterrent that frequently holds people back and often keeps us stagnated in life. How often have we heard something to the effect, "So many go to their graves without having used their natural born gifts/talents?" And, of these people how many use excuses such as, "I'm too young to start seriously thinking about my future because my parents always tell me to enjoy life while I'm still young..." Or, "I'm too old to try to do something new." While there may be some truth to these statements, one must not allow these mindsets as reasons to hold them back from at least initiating a plan towards tapping into his or her natural gifts/talents.

Some of us give up because we feel as though we didn't make wise choices in our youth and therefore are left with the consequences of "settling" as opposed to following our passions. Settling for some may mean going to a job every day that they hate. For others, it could mean not finishing high school or college. Yet and still, some of us, in our early teens and older, may rely solely on the government for assistant living without any plans of self-reliance.

I mention these not to judge as I am in no position to judge anyone. (I'm also sensitive to those that have to rely on government assistance due to illness.) I mention these because neither do you need to worry about aging nor settle for a lifestyle of UN-fulfillment! I'm not saying that it is easy to follow your talents. I'm definitely not saying it is easy to get anything worth having; but I am saying that anything worth having is worthy of pursuit by you and you are never too old, or in many cases to young, to just go for it!!

So, the question arises: what qualifies me to write on the topic of age with respect to not using your age as a deterrent in your life's journey? The short answer is: my life's experience, my 15+ years of ministerial experience and I also possess a MA, Biblical Studies – not to mention the array of people, teens and adults, that I've helped discover their hidden potential. What initially seemed impossible for them later became possible after they engaged in one-on-one conversations with me and received favorable results that enlightened them as they learned how to live out their dreams through tapping into their own self-worth by first altering their negative mindsets.

Unfortunately, discouragement frequently comes because of the ads we see where young strapping males with unbelievable pecks glisten or, slim shapely females with long flowing hair wearing outfits that leave little to the imagination seem to flaunt their youthfulness and beauty. Intellectually we know that sex and youth sell, right? And although outward appearances reign high in our youth-obsessed society and are highly praised, this mindset is a contributing factor as to why I felt compelled to write *This Side of Forty*: young people under 25 may feel as though they have all the time in the world to "get it together" and this is a gamble especially as we consider that none of us know with absolute certainty how many years we have left on the planet.

Yet many of us who have long since left our teens, twenties and perhaps our thirties, yearn to be younger, even if on a subconscious level. We somehow convince ourselves that only if we were younger we could have the things we now crave in our later years. In fact, I'd be rich if I had a nickel for every time I heard someone say, "If only I could go back to when I was young but with the knowledge and experience that I now have…" We must not feel inadequate about pursuing dreams at any age. Neither must we feel inadequate about aging! Sure, the ads we see are constant reminders of how fun youth *seems* to be; however, we must all recognize that no matter how beautiful youth is it will never match the *wisdom* and *experience* of the matured. We must not be discouraged or negatively influenced by the reality of aging because contrary to how high society may view youth, aging is inevitable for everyone but more importantly, aging can be as beautiful as the rising sun, or as enjoyable as a vintage bottle of wine!

It's all good. We don't have to bellyache over what we should have, could have done in our youth. But, before I continue, let me "holla" at the 35-year old and under group: this book is not just for people over 40! Y'all can also gleam some wisdom from these words. In fact, decisions made during your youth will definitely affect your future so please consider how to work the upcoming words in the following chapters to your benefit as well.

It doesn't matter where you are in your life or what age you are, NEVER EVER GIVE UP! I truly believe we can all achieve contentment to the point where we no longer have to desperately pursue it. Contentment can be as natural as breathing. What we must do is identity what makes us tick then learn how to make that identification into a reality. Sounds possible but not probable? Then you must keep reading. I don't promise to hand you happiness on a silver platter. I promise to give perspective with the goal of encouraging you to consider what might seem to be an impossibility to you could become your reality even if you're past 40. Therefore, if you're feeling stagnant or hopeless my goal is to bring hope and share that no matter where you are you can enjoy life and appreciate your age as well as pursue your talents at any age. Yes, even in this youth obsessed society!

Please email me after you've read this book to let me know the positive values it added to your life. For those of you that have less than positive feedback please put it in the form of a question. For example, don't say "I hate the points made in chapter 4." Instead say something like, "Why did you say such and such in chapter four?" Or state why you disagree with a point. I ask this because my goal is to encourage you; however, if you've read something other than encouragement or if something feels unrealistic to you I'd like the opportunity to defend my statements or have you shed light about a different outlook. Either way we both stand to gain something positive through sharing with integrity.

I reiterate no matter where you are in life stay encouraged. This can be challenging especially when there seems to be a "Murphy's Law" in effect with respect to where you currently are. Please give chapter 9 special attention if you believe you're a victim of Murphy's Law.

Nevertheless, if your life is already great and you're content as well as feel you don't need what's in the following pages please bless someone else that may not be as fortunate as you by recommending this book to them as a gift. It may be the blessing they need; yet you'll get the credit for sharing it with them.

Lastly, whether it is in your careers, relationships, or the simple rut of an unwelcomed daily routine, you can pursue your passion at any age. Everybody without exception has a gift and everybody without exception ages; therefore, you might as well explore the pursuit of what excites you! Either way, love ya!! –Cathy.

# PART I

*Perspectives*

# Chapter

# *One*

## What Do You Think Is
## Holding You Back?

*B*lame is easy. Sometimes it seems reasonable to blame others for our situations. Sometimes it is even reasonable to blame unforeseen situations for our misfortunes. This is what I have to say regarding whether or not it is justifiable to blame others or adverse situations as reasons why we have not accomplished our goals or obtained the lifestyle we desire: Knock It Off! Blame, as well as regret, is a useless emotion that cannot change whatever has already taken place.

Sounds mean? It is not mean yet the truth of the matter is that no amount of blame, regret, or justification is going to change our situations. Two people immediately come to mind: Oprah Winfrey and this writer. I'll start with Ms. Winfrey (who by the way I have much respect and admiration).

My confession is that I've never read her biography. My points come from following her talk show and interviews she's given. She came from the humblest of backgrounds. This is a mini recap of her life: she grew up poor, her parents separated when she was young, she was molested and raped more than once during her childhood, she did not grow up with a mother that encouraged her and she especially did not grow up being told she was beautiful. To add insult to misery she got pregnant outside of marriage while still a teen but lost the baby. She essentially grew up in a negative home environment. The odds she overcame are just unreal to the naked eye but she did it! If anyone has a reason to blame others for their misfortune it is Oprah. This is why she is one of my "she-roes." She overcame obstacles and adversity and later in life became the wealthiest black woman in America. And, she understands the concept of giving back and helping others. I love her story and have great admiration for her. Gayle is not her best friend in my mind. I'm her BFF, lol!

I had more advantages than Oprah in terms of coming from a two-parent working class household. My parents did the best they could with me yet it still wasn't enough to catapult me to achieving my goals during my teens and early twenties. They did not nurture my God-given gifts. I don't blame them for the outcome of my decisions; neither do I blame them for whatever was lacking in their parental skills. Blame, as previously stated, is in my opinion a useless emotion. I haven't always known this but this is what I now believe.

Here's a recap of the early stages of my life: my mother married my stepfather when I was about two so with all intent and purpose he's the only father I knew growing up. My natural father lived in the same city as me but for reasons beyond my understanding he never reached out to me. I met him at least twice in my life because my mother took my older brother and me to visit him when I was about seven years. I liked him. He tried to get me to call him "Daddy" but I laughed and referred to him by his first name. In my mind Daddy was at home on 71st

Street. What did I know? I was only seven! Maybe my natural father felt I was more content with the one I called "Daddy." I never resented him for not trying to get to know me – I'm sure he had his reasons.

A neighbor told my mother about the Catholic school about a half of mile from where we lived. I completed kindergarten and first grades at the nearest public school but transferred after a bad experience with my first-grade teacher who by any standard should not have been allowed to instruct little kids! The teacher whose class I transferred to at that school was extremely nice to me – so much so that I wished she could have followed me to every grade I advanced to throughout my entire elementary education.

Second grade was the beginning of my parochial education. Even the first college I went to fell under the umbrella of the archdioceses. My parents were great during my elementary years mostly because of my impressive grades that consisted mostly of A's and a few B's in my least favorite courses i.e. science and geography. Math was okay until about the eighth grade. My life changed drastically when I was fifteen and in my third year of high school.

I attended an all-girl private high school and was ready to transfer after my second year but my mother wouldn't hear of it. I vowed that if I were ever stupid enough to have kids I wouldn't force them to go to a school they absolutely hated and I'm happy to report that I've kept that promise, but I digress.

Please note that I promise this isn't an autobiography; however, I feel as though I must share the following details, which hopefully will enable readers to understand the point of this chapter.

I had few close friends during high school, was socially awkward and had low self-esteem. To say that I was miserable at that time of my young life was an understatement. My parents became unbearably strict most likely because I showed an interest in boys. I had as much freedom as I wanted until I went through that boy crazy phase that started at 13. What's worse is that my parents belittled me, dad more frequently than mom.

Mama, Dad and I were coming from the store early one Saturday afternoon. It was usually fun to hear grownup conversations but the conversation my parents discussed only minimally held my attention, at least until they said something funny or unfamiliar. They talked about how some guy from Dad's job got canned. My mother said, "I knew after the last time he was late that it was 63rd in Stony for him!" My attention was mostly diverted as I enjoyed the ride by looking at the sites outside the car window – passersby and pretty houses. I broke into their conversation and asked what did "63rd in Stony" mean. My mother shook her head and sniggled to Dad, "That girl is so dumb."

My nine-year old heart sank as I wondered to myself what had I done to deserve to be called "dumb" especially considering I was practically a straight A student. Mama explained that 63rd Stony Island was the end of the L train line that during that time went to Jackson Park, a southeast Chicago neighborhood. This was around circa 1975 when one of the L train lines in Chicago ran through downtown Chicago to Howard Street at the Evanston border from 63rd Ashland which was the southwest side of the Englewood community – the A train. The other Howard line that ran from Howard Street to 63rd Stony, which was the southeast side of the Jackson Park community – the B train. I had taken the A train many times but was oblivious to the B train so in retrospect I inwardly felt I knew who the actual "dummy" was since there had never been a need for me to be familiar with a route I never took. In other words, why should

I have been expected to be familiar with the B line which I'd never taken as opposed to the A line which I had frequently taken and was thoroughly familiar? Furthermore, should the mindset of a nine-year old be astute about trains? Especially considering she was usually chauffeured by her parents. Daddy laughed as I sunk lower in the back seat with hurt feelings. I wanted to cry. My parents inadvertently taught me how to internalize and harbor hurt feelings. I wasn't yet in the double digits and therefore did not know how to communicate my pain. I was paralyzed with shock by how my parents made me the brunt of their mentally cruel joke that emotionally burned me. I cried in the inside and was silent for the duration of ride. My parents seemed oblivious of the effects of their belittlement towards me.

Parents, guardians, teachers, summer camp aides, etc. please do not belittle children even if you're joking. Although nowadays kids are seemingly smarter than previous generations this doesn't mean their emotional maturity matches an adult. I don't believe my mother, God rest her soul, purposely tried to hurt my feelings. I believe she had been the object of ridicule while growing up or Dad belittled her and it trickled down to her children. I also believe she and Daddy were recipients of negativity and therefore translated those negative emotions to my siblings and me.

My father pumped me up as long I maintained an A average in school. Heaven forbid I struggled with a challenging class (high school chemistry) I would be harshly talked about and punished. I believe if I was encouraged to study harder, received special help by a tutor and told that things would get better I would have overcome my latter academic woes because knowing that my parents loved me no matter what would have been music to my ears. Instead I became rebellious and angry.

I began to exude cowardice behavior and lacked confidence. Sad, sad, sad!

It may seem that this trip down memory lane has strayed away from the chapter's title but it hasn't. I could take these early memories and blame my parents for everything wrong in my life from childhood to now (I'm a full-fledged adult with a husband and college aged sons of my own) but I don't blame them. The condescending comments that my parents expressed towards me could very well be a contributing factor as to why I'm the way I am but it is not the end all of who I've become... who I am.

I believe that even as a child I spent way too much time internalizing and not enough time playing up my strengths or even believing that I had strengths. I'm no longer a child and I must not be guided by anything negative from my past UNLESS I'm taking the negative and turning it into something meaningful and positive.

For years it was me who was holding me back! I felt that everybody else's was better than mine. I didn't have the confidence and/or self-motivation that Oprah must have had in her early years. I failed at everything I attempted including many friendships. Don't get me wrong, I was and still am a good friend. I've even maintained lifelong friendships to this day; but from the teen years until now I've encountered people that don't value my friendship by mistaking my kindness for meekness, which can ultimately be mistaken for weakness. Meekness which is a part of our makeup isn't necessarily a bad thing until our inherent meekness is mistaken for a floor mat.

The numerous failures I had actually helped me. I learned what I didn't like, which enabled me to narrow the choices of which path to take. There were many fields that piqued my interest but the top three areas of interest were: helping others, writing and interior design – all of which I am doing in some capacity. Please understand that one can truly do things they enjoy for others (and themselves) WITHOUT being financially compensated. I help people all of the time; sometimes I'm compensated, but more often than not it's on a pro bono or volunteer basis which in some ways is more satisfying because I do it from the heart.

I journal, which makes me a writer…at least in my mind it does, lol. I write because writing for me is therapeutic. In fact, writing was the one aspect of grad school I didn't mind (pulling all the research together is what was oftentimes tedious). I had a lightbulb moment and thought, "Wait a minute…since I like to write I may as well write something that could help others," enter *TSOF*.

I mentioned that I have an interest for interior design. I'm no professional designer but I frequently rearrange the furniture in my house which makes me feel like a decorator. My point is that we don't have to immediately earn massive amounts of money doing what we enjoy. We may find that doing things we enjoy until we learn how to transition them into our livelihood is an excellent way to enjoy the journey, without excuse, until the dream manifests.

Another excuse that leads the pack in keeping one stagnated is finances. Have you ever heard any of the following excuses or reasons? "I would go back to school but I don't have the money;" "I want to start my business but I don't have the money." Lack of finances is quickly followed by, "I would go back but I don't have time because of my work hours." "I don't want to go to college because I know lots of people with a college education that don't work in their fields." "I can't go back because I have a baby." "They always give the promotion to a white person before me." "I'm too sick." "I'm too tired." "I'm not smart enough."

"I don't know how to do it." "I'm too old." Sounds familiar? We can always make excuses or reasons not to do or attempt to do something that could propel us towards our goals. We must instead change this mentality and substitute it with the "I can do it" mindset. It's easier said than done yet nothing will happen if we just sit, complain and do nothing to change our current situation.

I attended several colleges and universities before I finally got my BA in 2002. Some people have a knack for obtaining scholarships for college expenses but I wasn't that person who knew how to get grants and free money to go back to school. My parents supported my first attempt at college with the condition that I had to become a nurse. I told my mother that I hated science and that I did not want to be a nurse! She forced me to be a candy striper at the local hospital that was located in close proximity to my high school. The only thing I recall liking is the cute uniform.

I told her I wanted to be a social worker yet she talked me out of it. She told me I didn't want to listen to people's problems all day long. I thought social work was commendable but got no support for it. The short of the story is that I flunked out of nursing school, started over at a community college and ended up at Columbia College-Chicago, which I absolutely loved.

I met who would later become my husband at Columbia, married six months after meeting him, but I dropped out of school due to finance. Five years into the marriage we had a son, then eleven months from that we had another son. I returned to Columbia when my youngest was two but my program was disrupted again due to lack of funds.

I moped around for years and was angry with my husband because he made too much money for me to get State grants yet he could not afford out-of-pocket costs. My fantasy was to attend school during the day while the kids were at school, then study after their 8:30 P.M. bedtime; but it was only a fantasy at that point. The reality was I could not afford to complete college and did not want to create more debt by taking out more than one student loan.

I started listening to sermons on prosperity and reading materials on the power of positive thinking. I determined within myself to stop making excuses, stop considering myself a realist; instead I started making excuses that turned my desires into my reality. It seems like as soon as I forced myself to change from having thoughts of defeat and replaced them with thoughts of victory, things changed immediately for the better.

Thankfully, one day on the way to the grocery store I heard a radio ad about UPS "Earn as You Learn" tuition incentive program and applied and got hired as a small-sort bagger at UPS. It was hard back-breaking work, but I kept my eye on the prize and stuck it out until I graduated with a BA from Columbia. My husband didn't necessarily like it but we also used a big chunk of our income tax return in order for me to complete my final semester because the tuition program did not cover the entire cost. He was attitudinal but at that point I didn't care because I had pussyfooted around with my education long enough so it was time to finally get my diploma. It was time for me to officially become a college graduate!

I don't deny that you may have a legitimate reason that is holding you back. You do not have to accept that as your permanent reality. Change your mindset! Don't be a realist! I had a neighbor once who was bellyaching over her financial situation. I tried to encourage her and recommended that she develop faith through prayer yet she responded, "I believe in God and everything but I'm a realist. Having faith won't change my situation." She was right, faith alone did not work for her,

BUT faith through a changed mindset worked for me! I'm not a zealous religious fanatic but I strongly believe that before anything changes for the better it has to start with a positive thought. I believe we can control how we think. Negativity will and always does rear its ugly head but we must meet it head-on and cut it off by replacing negative thoughts with positive thoughts. If you wait for things to automatically get better you might have a long and indefinite time to wait. On the other hand, if you decide to change your thought process change will undoubtedly happen. It first starts with change of thought; secondly you must put that change of thought into action.

One way to be proactive is to be determined to find resources to help you. This could mean not being afraid to ask for help for some. For others, it could mean researching how to accomplish a specific goal. The Internet is an asset and convenient research tool. However, everybody doesn't own a computer; but everybody can apply for a public library card then once issued, use a public computer to access the I-net for free. Do the work! Turn off that damn TV, get off your butt and do your homework. Don't be that person who wants the lime life but does little or nothing to obtain it. You want it handed to you on a silver platter but that isn't practical unless you happen to be a trust fund baby (and it's my understanding that wealthy people also instill work ethic into their heirs – can you say K-A-R-D-A-S-H-I-A-N-S?). Besides, do you really think you'd appreciate wealth or your dream job if it came that easily? The answer is no you would not! We've all heard the stories of how million-dollar lottery winners end up filing for bankruptcy because they did not educate themselves on how to properly invest their money. It grieves me whenever I hear this because I promise you that would never happen to me! Furthermore,

I never say "never" but I say "never" to this because the first thing I'd do is connect to Suzie Orman or some other reputable finance professional for advice. Plus, I would take the necessary steps towards educating myself on how to invest my money including enrolling in structured financing and accounting courses as well as initiate conversations with others that are successful in handling their finances.

Do you come from humble beginnings such as a poor urban community? If yes, do you believe your life could be better if you grew up in Beverly Hills or if your parents had a higher income, or if you lived in a safer neighborhood? We learned from Oprah that a humble beginning is no excuse; and I'm here to tell you that I've encountered many who grew up in Chicago's Cabrini Green, you know, the poor community where the '70's television sitcom *Good Times* is based, and now have successful lives including lucrative careers and live in desired neighborhoods. The current day Cabrini Green has been gentrified and most if not all of the projects and row-houses have been redeveloped into beautiful condos or homes. What was once a drab looking area has been transformed into a prosperous haven that includes businesses, boutiques and nice restaurants.

One friend of mine grew up in humble Cabrini with ten siblings, went to college on a full scholarship with no support, financial or otherwise from her family, and now has a dream job and lives in downtown Chicago in an area that is walking distance from Lake Michigan. Not too shabby for someone who grew up humbly or disadvantaged?

Another friend of mine that has eight siblings also grew up in Cabrini Green during her formative years but family later moved to Calumet Park, a south side Chicago neighborhood that for the most part is still easy on the eyes aesthetically speaking.

Anyway, several of her siblings have phenomenal careers and all are college educated. Not one of them is unemployed but looking at this family from the outside one might imagine that at least one would be a failure especially since they did not grow up in financial abundance, nor were they rich. Oh, by the way, neither scenario was on public assistance.

A final scenario is of a young man I haven't personally met but a good friend of mine shared his story with me about five years ago and the memory of it is still prominent in my mind. Let's call him "Jamal." Jamal lives in urban Chicago in a gang infested community where the school system leaves much to be desired. Both parents end up in jail before he completes elementary school. He's shifted from relative to relative until the release of his mother who is out of prison for less than two years before overdosing on heroin. Jamal's extended family deserts him and he floats through the State system until his second year of high school when his grandmother allows him to live with her. He vows to himself to make something of himself and focuses all his energy on academics. His teachers love him because he absorbs information like a sponge and never causes any problems. His grandmother appreciates the fact that he seldom expresses interest in going outside with friends but he'd rather spend his time participating in all things academic. He applies and gets accepted into several ivy-league universities. But here's the thing that most impressed me about Jamal: he turns down the acceptance to the State schools which for him would have meant free tuition since technically he's a ward of the State. With the aid of the Internet he applied and received over $80,000 in academic grants and scholarships! It gets better. All he has to do to keep the scholarships is maintain a B average. Jamal did not own a computer laptop, or tablet when he took advantage of finding grants. He took advantage of his grade school's dilapidated computers, frequented the Chicago public library where he set up a free email account and searched the Net for free. How's this for inspiration? Here's a young kid that could have succumbed to street gangs, dropped out, or ended up a weed head but he was determined to beat the odds and overcome his environment instead of living in a perpetual state of depression or feeling sorry for himself, which is the route that most of us take when things are tough. Where was Jamal when I needed free tuition? Lol!

We could argue that some people are destined for great things. Perhaps this is true; nevertheless, I maintain that what's good for the goose is good for the gander and both geese and ganders can have the determination to try to accomplish any goal where they direct their focus. Jamal may be considered an anomaly yet even as a young teen he positioned himself to focus. I bet he never stopped to think, "There's nothing I can do to help myself. All I can do is move in and live with whoever will have me and do what I'm told without giving voice to my pathetic situation." I don't know for sure what he told himself for inspiration but what I know is that he focused his attention on doing better for himself without letting his young age prohibit him from taking control of the few things he could control – for him it was doing well in school and researching opportunities. I love this kid who I'm sure is now an adult somewhere living his dream.

Another situation is of a lady I met at a church I used to frequent. She, her husband and five children relocated to the United States from overseas. She was a stay-at-home mom with a beautiful personality but never worked a job outside of being a domestic goddess or stay-at-home mom. Life threw her a curveball. Her cad husband left her to raise the children on her own. I'm talking desertion in the true sense of the word.

She was panic stricken and clueless about how she would provide for the children. One of the church members (not me) took her and all five children in until she got on her feet. She cleaned homes and babysat to earn money which helped but wasn't enough to survive on or adequately provide for her kids. One of the ladies she babysat for wanted to get her hair done in a carefree style that looked nice and enabled her to go swimming without having to fuss with her hair afterwards. She offered to braid her hair free of charge because she felt it was only proper to do something nice for someone else since so many people had extended kindness to her and the five, including free room and board. It also felt awkward to charge someone to braid hair which came easy for her since she had to braid her own daughters' hair.

The lady's hair was styled into beautiful French braids, also known as corn-rows, and she received so many compliments. Before you knew it the lady whose husband had deserted her developed a clientele and today owns a salon where she makes a handsome income braiding hair and doing hair extensions. This is a classic story of how someone received lemons and turned them into lemonade. She was thirty-six years young when her husband left her but considered it shameful to return to her home country. She is not wealthy but she and the children are comfortable. And, she never charges the people who helped her. Plus, she gives free hairstyles to underprivileged girls that want a professional hairdo for special occasions. I just love happy endings!

What do the aforementioned scenarios have to do with age? Or one's passion? Everything! We oftentimes use age as the reason to hold ourselves back. Instead, take time to think about the things you have. Find that silver lining. Know that you cannot find it if you're constantly comparing yourself to what others have, or if you're constantly thinking there's no way you can do better for yourself. Develop a burning desire to have whatever it is that you want as long as it's legal and appropriate. Disappointments will surface but don't let them become a deterrent. LIFE UNMISTAKABLY THROWS CURVEBALLS. There are people who seem strong or smart enough to know how to pick themselves up by their bootstraps and overcome obstacles. There are others that are perceived as too weak or stupid to overcome adversity. Whenever you feel as though you fall somewhere inside this spectrum you must never consider yourself weak or stupid especially when situations become difficult. Independently overcoming obstacles is great if it can be accomplished without becoming embittered. Many have crossed my path and have amazing stories of triumph; yet they are hard, distrusting and seem to be devoid of the ability to enjoy life and live it peacefully even though the threat is over. Not my hair braider! She and her children continue to thrive and enjoy life.

Others are too embarrassed to share their pain or seek help. They live in a perpetual state of misery and disappointment, which is sad. It's unfortunate but I've met people that are comfortable living in misery or non-victorious lives. It stands to reason that for them misery is the new norm. I hope not! This is the one time I'd welcome being wrong in my assessment. No one should consider living in misery or living in defeat as a permanent state.

One doesn't have to be smart or strong to overcome obstacles. One has to be willfully determined and driven to improve their circumstances. One must listen to that still inner voice which never disappoints!

I know sometimes it's difficult not to look at what others have accomplished and yearn for what they have especially when it's right in front of you; therefore, turn it into a positive if you must look at what others have. I have a friend who worked jobs paying minimal wage but admired her sister-in-law who was a well-dressed administrative assistant. My friend took typing courses in high school and decided to go to secretarial school after she witnessed how sharp her sis-in-law was. She got a job before she finished high school and today, three jobs later, my friend has advanced in her position with one of the leading airlines in the country and has travel benefits galore, but she started off as a typist. She looked at someone else in admiration then later made it happen for herself. Coodles to her for a job well done! Double coodles for offering me buddy passes!!

A little bit of determination accompanied by good work ethic can go a long way. The truth of the matter is that many of us (myself included) have hundreds of wonderful ideas but lack in bringing these ideas into fruition. For me, it's focus. I swear to you I may have had adult attention deficient disorder because I was that person who started one thing before finishing another and didn't do any project well. I was also that person that either couldn't make up my own mind or I'd let others influence my thinking. I also lacked skills in execution, which means you can be the best at something but if you don't know how to bring it all together into something cohesive you may not reap the benefits of your skills. I'm here to tell you not to give up! Instead learn how to recognize your strengths and weaknesses. Connect to someone that is strong in an area where you're not – perhaps this will enable a partnership that could be beneficial to both. Or even if having a partner doesn't appeal to you, you can still benefit by at least recognizing the areas of your skills that need to be developed.

For whatever reasons, there are people on this side of 40 and on that side of 40 that have not learned how to locate strengths and weaknesses. Be truthful with yourself and acknowledge your strengths as well as shortcomings because how else can you appreciate where you are in life, no matter what age you are, if you cannot be honest with yourself?

Some may consider age to only be a state of mind. I might have mixed feelings about this belief because there are some physiological changes that occur at specified times in our lives that undeniably age the body and force the state of our minds to change as well. For females, it's growing pains when our boobs start developing or when we start our menstrual cycle. Many of us suffer with monthly cramps too, yuck!

Menopause for some women is viewed as a cruel trick of nature. Was it not enough to suffer the woes of monthly cramps only to experience night sweats and uncontrollable mood swings that occur during the change? There's no escaping menopause! One way or another every female that makes it to seventy years of age has experienced menopause; the exception to the rule may be women that undergo a partial or full hysterectomy. Those of you that had a partial hysterectomy may not get the full-blown menopausal experience but whatever experience you had that caused the necessity of the partial hysterectomy (fibroid tumors or other common female issues) suggests that you only narrowly escaped the inevitability of menopause. Even with a partial hysterectomy your body was force to go through something and that something you went through occurred as you aged.

Women that undergo a full hysterectomy experience instant menopause and this happens at any age the full hysterectomy is performed. My advice is that all women should embrace the menopause process because once it's over you'll never have monthly discomfort again assuming there are no apparent or unforeseen physical issues.

Males, like us females, also experience physiological changes due to aging. Males may recall the experience during that awkward voice change phase when their voices fluctuated between sounding hoarse, high, low or girly until a developmental octave became permanent.

Men, remember your first wet-dream? Okay can we keep it real for a minute? You had no control over your nocturnal emission yet it's my understanding that most males experience their first by age 13. On the contrary, males have also been known to lose physical vitality as they age that for many starts after fifty; but thanks to erectile meds this no longer has to be an issue. Whew-hoo!

Trust that you can overcome whatever you think is holding you back from accomplishing fulfillment or whatever you believe will yield the kind of joy you desire to have in life. Above all, to the young or older, do not allow your age or life's obstacles to be the reason that you don't go for yours. Please keep reading!

# Chapter
## Two

## Reasonable Goals: No Goal Is Unrealistic...

*J* don't know about you but sometimes I get tired of hearing about the significance of setting goals, how to achieve fulfillment, get rich quick schemes, self-help, etc. It all seems like bull*#@*. Oops! Forgive the explicit but it's exactly how I feel oftentimes particularly when I consider how extremely successful people make it sound easy OR they overemphasize the importance of work ethic when you and I know numerous people that possess impeccable work ethic but are miserable... unfulfilled...and of course aging.

Conversely, one point I appreciate hearing from wealthy people is about the mistakes they made during their journey to richness. One wealthy person who shall remain nameless immediately comes to mind. He stated during a television interview something to the effect that although he made some mistakes along the way during his climb towards success, some people were mean to him throughout his journey; but he learned what not to do after some unsuccessful attempts at becoming the tycoon he is today. This isn't to say whether or not I'm a fan of this individual. A point well-made is a point well-made; making mistakes is where learning and growth take place so I'll give the wealthy props for this info in appreciation of a point well made.

On the contrary, a familiar cliché that annoys me is when I hear wealthy people say that being rich does not make you happy. While I believe this to be true I still inwardly think, "I bet you I'd be happy, fulfilled and all that other crap if I were wealthy!" I continue my inner monologue, "Besides, it's easy to say money won't make you happy when you in fact have lots of it. A**holes!" I realize this sounds negative but it isn't. In fact, it is simply impractical and/or naive for the wealthy – whether nouveau riche or vieux riche – to expect the working class and poor folks to simply believe money won't make you happy without having experiential knowledge for ourselves.

With this said, like it or not we working stiffs must set goals. Goal setting can be considered a necessary evil, or a necessary tool – it's doesn't matter how one labels it, goal setting must be done because it's an integral part of planning one's life along with determining where an individual expects to be at a specific age in life. If goal setting is something you're sick to death of hearing about but deep down inside know it's necessary, consider this: were you ever successful in an area you're most proud of without setting goals that catapulted your success? If your answer is yes skip the remainder of this chapter and go to the next chapter.

However, if you answered no because you know if you had set goals and implemented a strategic approach, you would have gotten that much closer to accomplishing your aspirations. I interject that goal setting is not synonymous with achieving success. Goal setting is the tool that can help you get closer to obtaining success but setting goals does not guarantee success; nevertheless, not setting goals can almost guarantee failure. Failure, by the way, is not always a bad thing. As implied earlier failure can be valuable when we learn from past mistakes. Yet avoiding as many mistakes as possible can also be a huge time saver. Everyone at all ages make mistakes – quite possible until the day we die. We should not be afraid of making mistakes, which is one thing that prohibits some from taking chances. Take a chance! Just avoid being frivolous in the chances you take and for heaven's sake don't repeat making the same mistakes over and over!!!

There are two categories of goals: realistic and incomplete-complete. Although the title of this chapter suggests another category of goals could be tagged unrealistic I don't believe in the existence of unrealistic goals because no matter how unrealistic a goal may seem it can ultimately become realistic if practical steps towards achieving the goals are taken; and assuming your goal isn't something that negatively affects others (i.e. if your goal is to murder someone so that you can steal their spouse, job, possessions; then you need professional help). Working towards something negative with an impure motive isn't goal setting it's sick! Goal setting that yields enrichment and fulfillment is what we should pursue. Besides, if you have to destroy someone else to achieve any type of success through goal setting that makes you an insecure person and valueless bully. And aren't there enough unscrupulous individuals in the world that live for the demise of others? Yes! So don't become that person, instead step into your own worth with integrity.

This brings me back to Oprah Winfrey. What were the odds of a poor black girl from the South (who grew up dirt poor, was molested by close relatives, got pregnant in her early teens and overall was a troublemaker) ever acquiring great wealth? Slim to none! But it happened and today she is known worldwide not to mention the fact that she is also a phenomenal philanthropist. I would say she is the epitome of what an unrealistic goal looks like if I believed in unrealistic goals; since I don't believe in unrealistic goals I contend that Oprah is the exemplification of what an incomplete-complete goal looks like.

Incomplete-complete goals are goals that appear unrealistic or impossible but they are the reality of what happens when an individual takes the time to set goals in measures of baby steps. Baby steps evolve into regular steps that evolve into giant steps that have the potential to evolve into phenomenal accomplishments. Amen!

Another situation where an incomplete-complete goal can materialize unexpectedly is when a naturally motivated person with excellent work ethic rises to the top seemingly without trying. Mark Zuckerberg, the creator of Facebook stumbled upon a pot of gold. Mark was a computer programmer at age twelve. What a blessing it is to identify one's gift so early in life. According to a CNN report Mark was a child prodigy when it came to computers: "Zuckerberg developed an interest in computers around 12 and used a basic messaging program to communicate within his father's dental office so that the receptionist could inform him of a new patient without yelling across the room. The family also used this program to communicate within the house. Mark also collaborated with his friends to create computer games just for fun. (CNN television broadcast)

"Facebook made the Fortune 500 list for the first time in May 2013, — making Mark Zuckerberg the youngest CEO at the age of 28 on the list." (Access Hollywood television broadcast)

The report went on to talk about how Mark's parents hired a tutor to help develop Mark's computer skills. Parents, see what can happen if you identify your child's interest early in life and support them? As a parent myself, I appreciate the encouragement Mark's father gave him by using the program Mark created in his dental business, which enabled him to be more discreet and professional towards his patients.

Before you begin to think that Mark was privileged since his Anglo parents were working professionals that gave him an advantage let's recall the childhood of Mrs. Beyoncé Knowles Carter. You must be living under a rock if you don't know who she is. It's my understanding from seeing televised interview clips and viewing various writings that she knew early in her childhood that she wanted to be an entertainer and frequently performed for family and friends; she also charged a modest entrance fee for the home concerts performed in her parents' basement. "As a child I knew I wanted to be an entertainer. I was always singing and dancing around the house. I always competed in pageants and auditioned for every play at school," Beyoncé recalls. (The Oprah Winfrey Show television broadcast 1997.)

Beyoncé attended private schools and dance classes; and perfected her powerful voice singing soulful hymns in the church choir. At age 8, she formed a pre-teen girl's singing group with sister Solangé and cousin/friend Kelly Roland. She performed with her sister and friend only later to become the pop trio, *Destiny's Child*, and is known world-wide! Of course, today Beyoncé is a solo artist. However, Beyoncé and Mark Zuckerberg alike, grew up with parents that recognized their talents as well as nurtured and supported them.

According to Beyoncé's extended family members, friends and neighbors also indulged her and sidekicks by financially supporting their talent even though back then it was on a small scale. Today Beyoncé, aka, Mrs. Carter, is a singer, dancer, song-writer, actress and fashion icon whose solo net worth is millions (which is independent of her income with famous rapper husband, Jay-Z. Collectively, I would not be surprised if together their worth is into the billions and counting). Phenomenal! Right? Imagine how it must be to make millions, perhaps billions doing what you love by following your passions.

Another scenario I observed was a young lady from afar who started off her career as a receptionist at a major hospital. She was organized, punctual and professional towards patients – even to those that waited in an eternally long line to see their physician. Once I attempted to butt the line to ask a question but she wasn't having it. She said, "Please go to the end of the line Ms. and wait your turn!" I told her I wasn't trying to be rude and only had one quick question to ask; but she wasn't having it and firmly sent me to the end of the line. Of course I was infuriated because truth be told, I was already late for my appointment and didn't want to risk waiting in that obnoxiously long line only to be told that I had to reschedule.

She must be showing off for the white people? Wrong! Over the years I've observed her and she treated everyone equally. I had been with my family doctor for years at that facility. Miss Lady got promoted. Not that I cared, but during a routine check-up visit I asked one of the receptionists where is "Little Dragon Lady?" the nickname I coined for her. I learned that "LDL" got promoted to what is equivalent to an office manager. I overheard coworkers say she was fresh out of high school and – assuming this is accurate she was most likely 18 years young, exuded professionalism, possessed an above average work ethic and moved up to a better position. I am not mad at her! I'm proud of her because her work ethic and integrity enabled her to quickly move up the administrative ranks.

This is how I see it. The other point for all I know is that she may have attended night or online courses that helped propel her to a better position. Either way, in my mind her attention to detail, great work ethic and professionalism across the board are the ingredients that aided in her climbing the ladder of success. From where I stand, some superior most likely recognized and appreciated her work style then promoted her to a better position with more responsibility.

Miss Lady's coworkers seemed to strongly dislike her. Patients have yelled at her too; yet this did not prohibit her from accomplishing her incomplete-complete goal. Whether she was overtly conscious of her ambition is inconsequential; the bottom line is that there is definitely something positive to be said about good work ethic, professionalism and integrity – all of which this young lady possessed.

For all I know she may have risen higher or perhaps moved to something altogether different. It doesn't matter – with this type of tenacity, motivation and courage she is another example of what the epitome of goal setting with favorable results looks like.

As I've already mentioned, Oprah likewise is perhaps the best example of an incomplete-complete goal. As a journalist by trade she is renowned for reaching goals and setting new ones. She has mastered dreaming new and bigger dreams. With Ms. Winfrey, there seems to be no time for complacency. She's an eagle. Eagles don't fly with flocks – they soar above the rest!

It would be remiss of me not to speak on young achievers who, unlike our greats discussed so far, already had post graduate degrees when they began their journey towards greatness. Co-inventors Larry Page and Sergey Brin started Google in

January 1996. It's my understanding that Google started out as a research project when they both were PhD students at Stanford University in Stanford, California. I feel compelled to mention the creators of Google because contrary to what many believe, college and graduate school are not obsolete. Moreover, these guys did not have startup money but they did not use lack of funds as an excuse to give up.

Personally, I love Google especially the search engine because it helped me with research throughout my time as a grad school student.

What's the moral of the aforementioned? Age has nothing to do with the habit of setting goals. Neither does age have anything to do with pursuing passions and dreams. Lady O and the receptionist turned office manager were young when they started their careers. We could argue that neither of them intentionally set goals and things just happened to turn out satisfactorily for both. I maintain that whether planned or unplanned it started off with making a decision to take a specific route, then apply the necessary steps towards accomplishing this by way of setting and achieving goals. I believe goal-setting has the potential to take one to heights that may not have necessarily been conceived in one's mind beforehand, but ultimately has the capability to exceed one's best expectation in her pursuit of following her passion; and this passion can most definitely be tied to one's livelihood. Goal-setting plus great work ethic is powerful.

Nobody could ever dissuade me from the significance of goal setting equipped with possessing an above average work ethic. These ingredients – goal setting and work ethic, are indiscriminate of race and economic background – and especially age!

# A Word to the Lazy

Do you know laziness is sinful? It's one of the 7-deadly sins. One doesn't have to be a Bible scholar to know this. It never ceases to amaze me how lazy people, at least the ones I've encountered, have a sense of entitlement. They won't get off their butts to attempt anything constructive yet somehow the universe owes them something.

I won't say how I know this person but let's just say I met her through mutual church friends. Let's refer to her as "Ms. Slothy." Ms. Slothy is highly intelligent, full of wit and has a strong personality. She also possesses a great sense of humor. She has six kids including two "baby-daddies." She lives with the latter set of children's father, but she doesn't work.

Ms. Slothy never holds down a job. She criticizes everything and everyone. She watches TV from sunup to sundown and she sits around all day in frumpy outfits. The one positive thing she does is pick her children up from school. Her housekeeping skills leave much to be desired and she raises her children solely on McDonalds.

So, what's my issue with Slothy? She misguides everyone that seeks academic advice for their majors and career paths through exaggeration of her own. She lied and said that she earned had a PhD. in medical science/biology and at the time no one had reason not to believe this lie that started in the early 2000's. Slothy claimed she worked as a medical researcher before deciding to go medical school to complete her residency. After she worked in a hospital for a couple of years, her exact position was never disclosed, she claimed the department head handpicked her to complete a coveted program where she earned credentials to become a medical doctor, or more specifically, a cardiologist, which was a lie from the pit of hell.

Fast forward to the recent past she asserted that she returned to school again and earned a second PhD in neuroscience. All boldfaced lies! It takes a bold person to lie about something this incredulous.

The son of a church member and mutual friend of ours applied and was accepted into a medical program. This friend, at the behest of Ms. Slothy, took a detour before applying to med school and instead influenced him to seek and receive a MA in psychology. This is commendable; yet how many people do you know attend a liberal arts program (Masters of psychology in this case) with the intentions of enrolling in med school? There are probably exceptions to the rule especially for those who desire to transition to psychiatry, but it's my understanding that most stick to traditional science related programs or research after obtaining a BA in science. Somewhere there was a communications issue but if I were a betting lady I'd bet you ten-to-one that Slothy gave horrible advice that led our mutual friend's son through this detour before he applied to med school. The mutual friend trusted and admired Slothy because of all she had *accomplished* especially considering these accomplishments came while raising six children. Most would agree that taking science related courses from any reputable university would have better than wasting time obtaining a degree that was not conducive for medical programs, prohibited him from generating a livable income in a beneficial field, as well as delayed him from attending med school. Slothy gossiped and said he'd never become a doctor.

Ms. Slothy speaks negatively about everyone! She was extremely jealous when our mutual friend's son was accepted into med school; and green with envy when our mutual friend graduated from med school at the top of his class! What's interesting is that everyone except Slothy is being productive with their lives. She has nothing except children (who are delightful) and a boyfriend; but no honest resources of her own. I grew up with the expression, "If you don't have anything positive to say about someone don't say anything at all." The ethers would be better off if Ms. Slothy applied this mindset. Apparently, it's much easier to bash others in order to somehow alleviate your lazy a**. Oops! Another language faux pas, I told you I'm not perfect. I just don't like to see the antics of others that are negative combined with taking advantage of the naiveté of someone else who's trying to be constructive with his life. And, for some it's easier to set someone up for failure, and later criticize them for failing. Unmotivated people find it easy to pinpoint the wrong in others who actually attempt to do something constructive with their lives. This may seem unworthy of being mentioned but it isn't. People should be more proactive in encouraging others instead of mocking or tearing them down.

This may seem harsh but I'm not judging! I'm witnessing the actions of another and have a low tolerance for deceit and negativity. I believe everyone has gifts OR untapped potential. I observed someone who has great potential but little or no motivation except to bash and condescend about others. Perhaps there's a lack of confidence or courage but one thing is for sure: no one ever knows what she/he can do until she/he actually attempts to do it. Maybe Ms. Slothy has attempted several endeavors unsuccessfully. This would substantiate why she's so bitter and misleading to others. Or, maybe the joke is on me? Maybe she enjoys sitting down eating Bon-Bons all day while watching soap operas. If this is the case perhaps I owe her an apology that would go something like this: "Ms. Slothy, I apologize if I've incorrectly judged or observed you. Who am I to determine your level of contentment and or fulfillment?

No one. Therefore, I humbly submit this apology but if you want a change in your life please stop talking negatively and misguiding others. Don't worry about your age either. You have time to set goals and develop a healthy work ethic. Please complete this book and hopefully you will gather some positive perspective that could help your untapped potential upon completion. Yours truly,

-Cathy with a "C." ☺

Are negative people in your life? What about naysayers? Please tune into the next chapter regarding a word to the naysayers!

# Chapter

# *Three*

## Naysayers

*O*ne should think twice about underestimating the power of positive thinking. I don't pretend to be an expert in this area but I know from personal experiences as well as from the experiences of others that there truly is power in thinking positively combined with having faith. Naysayers exist; however, we must learn how to activate our own faith that first starts with possessing a positive mindset throughout our journey and become victors of our own destiny.

Years ago, when I was about two years into my marriage I had the pleasure of attending one of Evangelist Kenneth Hagin's workshops during his visit to Chicago circa 1988. He delivered a powerful sermon that included an illustration of how he overcame a fatal disease that practically killed him when he was young. Diagnosed with "a deformed heart and an incurable blood disease" from birth, Hagin was partially paralyzed by age 15, confined to bed, and told he had little time to live. Many don't overcome one of these dreadful diseases let alone two; thankfully, he beat the odds and conquered both diseases. Medical professionals did not expect him to see his tenth birthday yet he was cured during his teen years and did not pass away until 2003 of natural causes at age 86. Here's what Kenneth Hagin shared during this conference: "My heart stopped in April 1933, and other vital signs failed three times. I felt myself being dragged to hell and prayed for Christ's help and forgiveness; and then came back to life. This miracle defined the rest of my life." (Kenneth Hagins Conference, DePaul University, Chicago 1988)

He quoted Mark 11:24 from the Bible: "What things soever ye desire, when ye pray, believe that ye receive them, and ye shall have them." By 1934, Hagin believed that he would be fully healed, and he was. (King James)

If you think this is some sort of ploy to convert you, you're sorely mistaken. I'm no evangelist and the purpose of this chapter is not to proselytize you. This directly ties in with positive thinking. Consider one of Hagin's most quoted passages of Scripture from the Christian Bible: "...Have faith in God. For verily I say unto you, That whosoever shall say unto this mountain, Be thou removed, and be thou cast into the sea; and shall not doubt in his heart, but shall believe that those things which he saith shall come to pass; he shall have whatsoever he saith. Therefore I say unto you, What things soever ye desire, when ye pray, believe that ye receive them, and ye shall have them." (KJV, Mark 11:22-24)

One must exercise positive thinking in order for prayer to work. Believers may call it having faith; religious skeptics may consider it as blind faith. Either way, whether praying or chanting affirmations, it all starts with training one's mind to hold positive thoughts which transitions to positive words which can ultimately manifest a positive outcome as in the case of Evangelist Hagin.

So, I attended the Kenneth Hagin conference in Chicago with some Christian friends. I'd been most depressed due to the news that one of my fallopian tubes was fully blocked and the other was partially blocked which meant that I could not conceive. This devastated me because I'd always believed that I was someday meant to be a mom by natural means.

I had done everything right in my mind – or at least in terms of first getting a husband, then having children. My older brother already had four kids with his wife and it just somehow didn't seem fair that they had four and we had none. Although my younger brother did not have kids at the time it was likely that he would someday have children without issue, and he does.

I'm giving Evangelist Hagin my undivided attention as he spoke something to the effect of, "They told me I was going to die when I was just a kid but I prayed and asked the Lord to give me a Scripture that says otherwise and I will believe with faith that my healing is on the way." He continued, "Folks, if you're believing God for something don't give up! Literally stand on the Word of God for what you're believing. I mean put that Bible on the floor and stand on top of it!!" (Kenneth Hagin Conference, DePaul University, 1988)

My husband and I had been married for over three years without getting pregnant. I asked my obstetrician if there was something he could do to help me (previous doctors gave no hope). He administered a prescription for a hormone that completely cut off my monthly cycle for six months. I got pregnant about two months after taking the hormones for six months BUT to my dismay I miscarried because the embryo had a low blood count. I knew something was wrong because I started spotting about seven weeks into the pregnancy.

The first impulse was to slip back into depression; but I spoke to the devil and call him a liar. First, Satan whispered lies that I could NEVER conceive let alone give birth. I told him, "I'm not listening to you! You said I would never get pregnant and I now know that I can in fact get pregnant." I prayed to God and said, "You say in your word to be 'fruitful and multiply' so what do you think we're trying to do?" This actually was not a prayer; in fact, in my frustration I was indignant with the Almighty (which by the way is not acceptable but due to grace and mercy God Almighty forgave my irate behavior). I told God that not getting pregnant and giving birth to a healthy baby was simply not an option for me.

I got pregnant about six months later and thirty-eight weeks after that I delivered a healthy baby boy! Guess what, his brother came eleven months later. Yes, our two sons share the same age for a couple of weeks. I joke and say that they're *Irish Twins*. (If you happen to be Irish/Catholic you may know what this means, lol.)

As you can ascertain, the power of positivity, through prayer in this case, definitely works! (Having a determined obstetrician didn't hurt either.) And, although I consider myself spiritual I don't consider myself to be holier than thou! I'm a flawed human being that's made many mistakes in my life. The one mistake I did not make was to doubt that I could never become a mother, which has been one of the most fulfilling experiences of my life! (Please view the poem at the end of this book written by me and inspired by my now college aged sons).

Another seemingly impossible situation is the story of Joshua and Caleb. Both accounts are found in the Old Testament and the Torah. (I feel compelled to relay that one does not have to believe in any religion to gleam wisdom from what's fundamentally regarded as holy and/or philosophical writings.)

Joshua and Caleb are two Israelite men whose stories offer an example of exercising faith. Both men traveled with the Israelites when Moses led them through the Red Sea and into the wilderness after being delivered from slavery under Pharaoh's Rule in Egypt. Joshua and Caleb were selected along with ten other men to explore the Promised Land and give a report to Moses and the people. After forty days of exploration in Canaan all the explorers except Joshua and Caleb had a negative report, "…We came unto the land whither thou sentest us, and surely if floweth with milk and honey; and this is the fruit of it. Nevertheless the people be strong that dwell in the land, and the cities are walled, and very great: and moreover we saw the children of Anak there." (KJV, Numbers 13:27-28)

This report frightened the people because the Anakites were descendants of the Philistines and giant-like in stature.

Caleb had a different attitude from the other spies. "And Caleb stilled the people before Moses, and said, Let us go up at once, and possess it; for we are well able to overcome it." (Ibid Numbers 13:30) When the people complained that they could not go up to conquer the land, both Caleb and Joshua responded strongly: "And Joshua the son of Nun, and Caleb the son of Jephunneh, which were of them that searched the land, rent their clothes: And they spake unto all the company of the children of Israel, saying, The land, which we passed through to search it, is an exceeding good land. If the Lord delight in us, then he will bring us into this land, and give it us; a land which floweth with milk and honey. Only rebel not ye against the Lord, neither fear ye the people of the land; for they are bread for us: their defense is departed from them, and the Lord is with us: fear them not." (Ibid, Numbers 14:6-9)

God judged the people of Israel by making them wait forty years to enter the land. He also promised that every person 20 years old or older would die in the wilderness and would not see the land with two exceptions—Caleb and Joshua. Why? Because the servant Caleb has a different spirit and follows God: "But my servant Caleb, because he had another spirit with him, and hath followed me fully, him will I bring into the land whereinto he went; and his seed shall possess it." (Ibid, Numbers 14:24)

Nobody except, Caleb and Joshua, gets to enter the lands flowing with milk and honey since they neither have a positive report nor maintain positivity through faith. "And the men, which Moses sent to search the land, who returned, and made all the congregation to murmur against him, by bringing up a slander upon the land, Even those men that did bring up the evil report upon the land, died by the plague before the Lord. But Joshua the son of Nun, and Caleb the son of Jephunneh, which were of the men that went to search the land, lived still." (Ibid, Numbers 14:36-38)

This promise came true. After the death of Moses forty years later, Joshua led the people across the Jordan River into the Promised Land. Caleb also received an inheritance in the Promised Land in his old age (KJV, Joshua 14).

We see how the faith of Joshua and Caleb teaches us that we are to believe in ourselves (and God) even when others do not believe in us. When we do this, we set ourselves up to receive great blessings.

My influence is not sealed only in Christian doctrine. I read the, *The Bhagavad Gita*, which in short is derived from Hindu doctrine and was translated to English by Sir Charles Wilkins c. 1785. *The Bhagavad Gita*, also known as *The Bhagvat-geeta*, which from this point forward I will simply refer to as *The*

*Gita,* is considered a well-respected scholar in many circles and reminds me of poetry, prose and even psalms. There is also wisdom to be gained through human struggle, among other points that may encourage growth and development as one ages and faced with difficult decisions.

*The Gita* makes noteworthy points regarding one's personal faith. In the first chapter Prince Arjuna is charged with defending his older brother's claim to the throne and receives help from the Lord Vishnu, the incarnated Hindu God, who fosters and preserves the universe against forces that try to destroy and corrupt the universe. Arjuna understands that war with his extended family is inevitable and his dilemma is the casualties that occur as a result of war, which in this case will be his cousins, uncles, and other family members that oppose him. *The Gita* is loaded with wisdom yet the focal point that reigns supreme for me is how one must exercise faith about life choices. The first chapter in *The Gita* is entitled *Lamenting the Consequences of War* (modern translations may be entitled *The War Within*); which is appropriately titled because it's all about the battlefield within the individual's mind and later we learn how the main character seems to feel better about the pressing decision he must make. Spoiler alert: Arjuna learns about the power of faith toward the end of the *Gita*: "...Krishna told Arjuna to look to the scriptures to guide his actions, so that he can avoid the lower road that leads backwards to a less evolved state." Now Arjuna wants to know about those who do not follow the orthodox way laid out in the scriptures and who nevertheless offer some kind of worship with faith in their hearts. In reply Krishna goes into great detail about [faith]. He also stresses the importance of *shraddha* or faith...We might say that our shraddha is the sum total of our values, what we really hold to be important in our lives. Every human being, Krishna says, is shraddha-maya, "made up of faith" – as the Christian Bible puts it, as we think in our heart, so we are (Proverbs 23:7).

The Gita also holds that no lasting progress is possible on the spiritual path without a great deal of self-discipline...and power gained through spiritual discipline. Krishna concludes that no act or intention can add to spiritual growth if it is faithless." (*The Bhagvat-geeta*, Sir Walter Wilkin, 1785)

Therefore, forget what the naysayers in your life think and say about your potential. No matter how old you are you must give birth to your visions and have faith in your abilities to bring them into fruition. Believe in you!

---- *Chapter* ----

# *Four*

## Spirituality and Age

*Y*ou don't have to be a born again anything to be considered spiritual. I think we can all agree that more and more science and spirituality (or religion) are merging or perhaps have already converged in some circles. Not only do most hospitals hire chaplains from various religious denominations to minister to the sick; they also have specialized programs designed specifically for the *Mind, Body and Soul* that frequently fall under the umbrella of holistic care. What's groovy about these programs is that no one is forced to partake of them – it's simply available for those that want it.

The question arises: what does spirituality have to do with age? The short answer is: probably nothing. So why interject spirituality? The purpose of this topic is to introduce a perspective for consideration. First I must warn you. If you feel as though there is nothing beyond life as you know it, that this life is all there is and you merely waist away after death; you will reject the following position; and should skip to the next chapter.

However, if you believe there is more to existence than what meets the eye I oblige you to continue reading this chapter. Remember, my goal is to share insights regarding why we mustn't use age as a deterrent in setting and achieving goals as well as pursuing our passions. It's important to share views that may or may not have been taken into consideration. My confession here is that as you may have already discerned I am influenced by various religious mindsets. (In fact, I believe all religions have common beliefs but that's for a different discussion.) I should also interject that we use the term "religion" when in fact we mean "spirituality." My opinion of the difference between the two is that one is bondage, dogmatic and ritualistic; unlike the other, which is free, incorporeal, ethereal or perhaps mystical – I'll leave it to you to decide which one is bondage or which one is freedom. My point is fundamental religious mindsets can serve as a guide to shape convictions without all the arguments that frequently arise whenever religion becomes the topic of conversation. With that said, keep in mind that these are only views for your consideration and not intended to proselytize you. Fair deal?

Please note my second caveat: there's no such thing as age in eternity. Age in eternity is contrary to age as we know it in this life. Some type of transformation takes place when people, places, plants and animals develop in our world. Humans and animals alike start off as babies and continue to grow for the duration of their lives. We may not grow taller after reaching adulthood but our features continue to change a little bit day by day. Now, let's explore a perspective regarding spirituality from the cosmos to the earth, which hopefully will draw us closer as to why we should not hold our age hostage as we dare to dream about life's possibilities regardless of our current age.

## The Big Bang Theory and More

The non-religious scientific mind believes that existence exploded into being via what has been coined "the big bang theory." I believe this is true; but I also believe "the big bang theory" is only part of the story:

One television evangelist said something to this effect, "How can an automatic explosion of planets fall into perfect place...it just doesn't make any sense..." The theory of the big bang phenomenon is only partially accurate because *Someone* would have had to be responsible for an explosion that landed the planets into perfect order including setting the earth on its axis.

Don't judge me but I viewed the 2012 concert of comedian Katt Williams entitled *Kattpacalypse*. Katt talks about the atheist vs. the Christian views in his comedy routine. He boldly states: "Just because you a Christian don't believe you can't believe in science. I believe in all the science... Science [don't] always makes sense. Then these...want to come up with some... that just don't make no...sense. Just two particles banged together – made this whole...planet with everything on the... right? Everything go together everything link up everything hook up everything perfect. [They]...want me to believe two atoms banged together [and] made this whole...world. If you believe that...tonight after the show go to the parking structure and bang on your car until it becomes a better car." (www.sho. com/sho/comedy/titles/.../katt-williams-kattpacalypse)

He made me laugh out loud at this mostly because my views are similar. Matter of fact, I would love to beat my hail-ridden Dodge Magnum station wagon into a beautiful new Lexus Truck! Yes, I believe in the Big Bang Theory; but as previously stated I also believe the BBT is only half the story and a Supreme Being was responsible for the natural order of the universe. Moreover, Pope Francis himself has shared his ideas regarding the convergence of science and religion with respect to the Big Bang Theory.

The Pope has admitted something to the effect that scientific theories are not necessarily incompatible with the existence of a creator and also that evolution in nature is not contradictory or a capricious notion of creation, because evolution requires the creation of beings that evolve. My sentiment also parallels the Pope's view.

I reiterate that my goal is to assist in broadening views, not to stir up controversy. We each have our ideas and opinions and it is okay to view other ideas that may differ from yours.

If we fast-forward from creation to current day we must accept that the earth has evolved and is not the same earth it was eons ago. By biblical standards the quality of the earth depleted and had no choice but to change because of the introduction of sin by humans, (see Leviticus 18:25). We might not agree with this but the fact remains: mistreatment of the earth, via sin or general abuse, causes irrevocable and detrimental harm. Can you say ozone layer?

The vastness of the universe generates hope of there being something further to look forward to – an afterlife of some sort. This life is a minute preview of things to come. You are not required to agree with this…the fact of nature is indisputable in that your body is physically dead way many more years than alive. I believe this in and of itself is reason to challenge a unilateral scientific mindset that suggests this life is all there is; perhaps we should at least consider an alternate nonscientific approach to all things spiritual.

But to be fair to the skeptics let's consider Charles Templeton, who use to follow Christian views on the age of the earth but later changed his mind and followed an agnostic view of evolution. Templeton had been a successful evangelist and was a contemporary of Billy Graham, who is also a well-known evangelist. However, despite his popularity as an evangelist, Charles Templeton discovered that the more he read, the more he questioned Christian faith and no longer trusted the biblical account of creation as found in the first chapter of Genesis.

In a conversation with his contemporary and fellow evangelist, Billy Graham, Templeton expressed his concerns and decided to attend seminary since at that point he had not formally studied theology. Templeton felt it was not possible to believe the biblical account of creation – he didn't believe the world was created over a period of days a few thousand years ago; instead, he believed the world evolved over millions of years. Argue whatever point you choose the bottom line for him is that he believed that creation ages through the process of evolution.

This brings me to the biblical explanation of creation/ evolution: What does the Lord Jesus have to say about the age of the earth? Christ interpreted as historical fact what people consider as myth and demonstrated that there is no higher source than Scripture that we can petition to as a source of truth (KJV, 2 Tim. 3:16; 2 Pet. 1:20-21). Christ also emphasized the perspicuity of Scripture. He says in the Gospels eleven times, "have you not read . . .?" and thirty times, "It is written..." He never adapted his teachings to the false notions of his audience, he knew the differences between the traditions of men and the truth of God's word and Christ spoke the truth because according to the Christian faith He was and still is the Truth (John 14:6). Jesus Christ also stated that belief in the writings of Moses were foundational to believing what He says in John 5: 45-47 which is directed to current day believers.

Finally then, we determine from Scripture that aging (and death) is the direct consequence of sin; moreover, creation itself was affected due to the original sin (Romans 8:20-22).

What does all this mean? How does it tie into the aging process? According to the Christian Bible aging (then inevitably death) truly is the direct consequence of the first sin. Christians believe it was not God's original plan for humans to be born, grow old, and then die. God gave humans freewill to choose. This means it is not God's fault that mankind chose to do wrong by sinning. If God forced us to do right we would not be humans; instead we would be robots. We could argue that God could have wiped the slate clean and created new and different humans that would have obeyed. The problem with this is that wiping the slate clean would have meant there was no chance of redemption for the original sinners, who would have been erased from existence, which likewise could be viewed as unfair. It could also suggest that during antiquity God was too passive to deal directly with disobedience; except God is not passive. God loves all humans and provides a way for deliverance (through salvation) that is solely left up to the human to accept or reject. There is no need to get into specifics because we've heard it all before. Besides, his righteousness is actually too great and just to allow sin to happen without providing salvation for the redeemable. For those that may not know what I'm referring to just ask your local priest/pastor. But I digress.

What it boils down to is that age in eternity is nonexistent. Subsequently, if you believe that humans will be given a glorified body in the afterlife, you will better understand these points. Assuming we have been administered this glorified body, also assume that once given it will not perish! 1 Corinthians 15:42-44 affirms this. And, it stands to reason that if our bodies will be raised to be imperishable then our bodies will also likewise be ageless. Yes and amen!

Age therefore is not our enemy; neither is it a deterrent to our goals, passions and purpose. Appreciating our age is synonymous to appreciating God and his gift to us which is life (and of course Salvation if you believe in Christian doctrine). Our gift back to God is the good we do with this gift of life. Moreover, honoring the gift of life at any age shows God appreciation. A further appreciation to God is how well we utilize all of our God-given gifts and talents.

A lack of appreciation is when we grunt and moan about not being able to do this or that because of age. Perhaps we are not mature or confident enough in ourselves to understand that we possess gifts and talents that we have the ability to develop. Although I've used Christian doctrine to support my points one does not have to be a Christian or religious to accept this truth. It's so easy to make excuses. It's so easy to hold unto negative thoughts that keep us from even trying. We simply must stop it! If all we do is moan and complain nothing for sure will be accomplished. We must understand the necessity of looking at the glass as being half-full.

It took me a long time to understand the power of positivity. I obsessed over what it would be like to be wealthy. I mean stinking rich is what I obsessed about; and the pathetic part is that I did little or nothing to do what it would take to become rich. All I did was fantasize about it. Don't get me wrong; everything starts with a concept...a dream...an idea. However, these thoughts must graduate and go from potential energy to kinetic energy lest the thought dwindles into nothing more than an insubstantial space in one's brain. We must seek and not give up. We must do. If we perform an action sooner or later something, good or bad, will happen. If all we do is daydream without acting or without doing any work we know for sure that nothing, positive or negative, will happen. It is called being stagnated.

Don't assume that if you activate your concepts that end up failing it was a waste of time. Greatness is more often than not birthed out of failure. Ask Thomas Edison. It's my understanding that Tommy failed thousands of times before he was successful at inventing the lightbulb. How many of us persevere after multiple failures? Many are ready to throw in the towel after only one or a few attempts. Can you imagine the frustration of Edison? He believed that after each failure he got that much closer to success. We've all heard, "believe in yourself..." which is true – it definitely helps to believe in oneself and to push forward. Edison understood the concept of believing in oneself well and I for one am glad he did not give up. What a fantastic mindset!

Let me interject this: move forward even if you are not fully confident in yourself! I say this because I observe wealthy people and many of them pound in our heads how necessary it is to believe in yourself, hard work, have discipline, perseverance and determination, yada yada yada. My take is that it is easy for them to say because they've arrived. Whatever problems they may have lack of finances is not one of them. Some of them seem to have lost sight of the fact that most cannot relate to them because the well to do have already reached their goals... they're wealthy. What could they possibly know about my situation? Sure, many of them were once where we currently are BUT for us it is still only a dream in progress. Many of us aren't necessarily looking for wealth – many of us just desire to know what it feels like to live our dreams out loud by earning a livable income that enables us to utilize our gifts and passions.

Please understand. There truly is something to be said about possessing excellent work ethic. I personally believe that strong work ethic can yield a myriad of success be it wealth or landing that dream job that pays well. But, how can we relate to work ethic etc. if we are struggling with bills? We must not try to relate to it. Instead we must develop a strong work ethic in an area that charges us. Whatever excites us, what we are passionate about is the very thing that we should not mind working hard at; and, if we continue to work hard success is inevitable and the bills will get paid. (This assumes that what we seek does not cause harm to others but empowers us as well as others.)

Furthermore, success does not always equate wealth. Success can be peace of mind. Think about it. What good is it to have wealth without the accompaniment of peace? Nothing! While we all have varying definitions of success I believe we can all agree that no amount of success in the world means much it we don't have peace of mind.

We must trust that once we position ourselves to enjoy our journey and find the very thing that brings us joy is all we truly need. Subsequent things such as increase of finances, material gain, etc., will be the icing on the cake. We should not obsess over riches or what other people have. What others have could be an illusion because we don't know with all certainty if their possessions equate fulfillment.

Years ago, I had a friend who married a guy that had a professional job, earned a professional salary, had a house built in a prestigious suburb and was easy on the eyes. She had the opportunity to select everything from floor designs to cabinet hardware. I was a stay-at-home mom at the time and had the opportunity to visit her without bringing the kids. In my mind we would spend the day mentally decorating the house, catching up on the latest gossip and simply enjoy our girl time together.

To my surprise she was miserable. I asked her how she could be so unhappy in this beautiful new home. At the time my husband and I lived in a two-bedroom apartment with our two toddler sons who shared a bedroom. It was a nice apartment in a nice neighborhood but it was not a brand spanking new six-bedroom house!

My friend responded, "It's hard to be happy in any house where your husband seems not to care about anything except his job. My friend had never driven a car, which meant she was dependent on her husband to chauffer her everywhere. Her husband felt bombarded to work all day only to be asked to be driven places upon arriving home.

Before moving to the burbs, she lived in an area that was convenient to everything – the grocery store, boutiques, entertainment places and cool restaurants. Also, city buses and trains were easily accessible if she wanted to visit a museum or local zoo. Everything was spread out in the suburb where she lived, which meant she had to be driven everywhere. I frequently offered to drive her places and tried to encourage her to get her driver's license but in retrospect I believe she may have been nervous about driving. She seldom took me up on my offer – I suspect my toddler children got on her nerves, which was probably the reason why she usually declined my offer.

Her husband was a nice guy but seemed to be devoid of personality and/or feelings. He was kind of dry. I understand that everyone isn't bursting with high energy but they were true opposites in the true sense of the word. His indifference and insensitivity seemed to devastate her to the point of unhappiness.

So you see, one could have a great home, no worries about money, pretty clothes and friends yet still be unhappy. Go figure.

I don't brag on much but I feel fortunate to know how to be content within myself. My income does not parallel Oprah's or Mark Zuckerberg's by any stretch of the imagination. I have a home that seriously needs to be updated. I don't drive a fancy car but would if I could. My list of have-nots goes further than my haves BUT that's neither here nor there; the point is that while I don't have every material thing I want I have joy, fulfillment and sometimes happiness. The times that I'm not happy is when I'm sick or a loved one is sick. Otherwise, I've always known how to make myself happy without being codependent on people or material things (shoes might be the exception).

From the time I was a young girl I learned how to adjust to the fickleness of others. Growing up I lived on 71st Street, which was a busy street and my parents didn't allow me to cross to the other side at will. I had to be adult supervised. Whenever my friends and I would play double-dutch, a jump rope game, I usually won. They'd get mad and cross the street leaving me behind because they knew my parents prohibited me from going. This only upset me for about three seconds. I told them, "Fine! I don't care. You're just mad because I won!" I'd take my rope, triple it and skip all the way home in victorious bliss due to the fact that I'd won the rope game. Usually I'd go inside and find something on TV to watch; or I'd go around the corner to see what the kids on the block behind me were up to because there were no busy streets to separate me from visiting the kids on 71st Place. Either way I made it my mission in life to stay happy.

I'm still this way today. I can honestly say that throughout my life there are only three people that have the ability to upset me to my core: my parents (now deceased); occasionally my husband and children. Even so, after I collect myself I decide not to allow the loves of my life to perpetually work my nerves. Truthfully, I may not be the best at dealing with personal conflicts as it pertains to interacting with my loved ones; however, I know how to get adversity out of my spirit... my inner being. In fact, I used to snap off at the drop of a dime when I was younger. Usually I'd either confront adversity or just walk away. For the most part, I've learned how to deal with conflicts without stepping out of character or without carrying the weight of somebody else's foolishness. That said, no one rains on my parade without my permission!

Be determined not to let other situations or people deter you in your quest to reach goals, find happiness or live in a perpetual state of joy. Neither should you be your own worst enemy by over thinking your age. Remember: there is no spoon. What do I mean? Have you ever seen the movie, *The Matrix*?

Long story made short, the main character, Neo (Keanu Reeves), lives in a computer-generated world called the matrix. He's tasked with fighting an army of sentinel agents known for being unstoppable. He visits the Oracle who serves as a guide. He witnesses a kid that bends a spoon with his mind as he awaits a meeting with the Oracle. One minute the spoon is bent, the next second it's erect. The kid tells him that it is impossible to bend the spoon. The kid says, "There is no spoon!" In other words, Neo was able to see the spoon as being bent because it was mind over matter, and since they were inside "the matrix," the spoon was nonexistent. Age is similar in that in this case there is no age...there is only one's state of mind.

# Five

## Hashtag: #AgeIsNothingButaNumber

We have no choice but to accept the aging process so why not just embrace it?! One clarifying moment regarding age came to me when my maternal grandmother (now deceased) told me, "Cathy, we are all graveyard travelers." She made this proclamation in her usual comedic tone yet at the same time she was serious. I only vaguely recall what led up to this truth. I believe we were watching television – perhaps *Lifestyle of the Rich and Famous,* which aired in syndication during the 1980's and 1990's. It's always fun for me to view how others live the life of luxury. One of the guests said something to the effect that they'd never want to live anywhere else than where they currently lived. I confessed to Mama Katie how lucky they were to live such fabulous lives except she did not seem overly impressed.

My grandmother, aka Mama Katie, countered, "Cathy, I imagine that mansions, Rolls Royce's, and jewels are fun but after all is said and done we are all graveyard travelers so it doesn't matter what you have in life, rich or poor everybody has a limited amount of time to enjoy stuff."

She was right! This was a clarifying moment for me because until then I had never considered how temporary this life is. I was about thirteen when we had that conversation. It seemed as though I had all the time in the world and would stay young forever. I came to a mental screeching halt. I thought to myself how hard it must be for rich people to give up this life unless they understand that this life can be viewed as a rest stop before we get to our eternal destination, a destination which I believe is wonderfully unparalleled to this life.

My newfound knowledge did not prohibit me from desiring nice things such as a nice car, pretty outfits and lots of shoes. Yet in the same vein our conversation taught me to be content whether or not I possessed things. Make no mistake, I frequently go to fantasy land in the crevices of my mind and wonder what it's like to be Oprah or Beyoncé – both who seem to have exciting lives and nonstop bliss. I am not naïve and know that everyone, rich or poor, have challenges in life. However, I've convinced myself that if you have God, health, people in your life that love you, life's essentials (food, clothes, shelter, water) and a good heart then you must have everything you need to be happy. Right?

Mama Katie used to say, "Happiness is in the dictionary!" She'd insist that I learn how to be content not happy. As an admirer of Scripture, I agree with what it says regarding joy, "...Ye love [Christ] whom, though now ye see him not, yet believing, ye rejoice with joy unspeakable and full of glory" (1 Peter 1:8). Also, "And ye now therefore have sorrow: but I will see you again, and your heart shall rejoice, and your **joy no man taketh from you**," (John 16:22). Joy can be present in the midst of storms; unlike happiness which is temporary, contingent on materialism and/or is codependent on circumstances.

Codependence that accompanies happiness can come by way of being codependent on a loved one. There's absolutely nothing wrong about enjoying our loved ones; we are supposed to love, receive love, as well as enjoy them. We run the risk of setting ourselves up for irreversible vulnerability if we tell ourselves that we cannot survive without a certain somebody. We must not set ourselves up to be overly dependent on someone else if for no other reason than the fact that life as we currently know it is temporary (or heaven forbid they precede us in death). And, while we figure that we know where our final destination in eternity will be (heaven) we don't necessarily know the destination of others including our loved ones.

Recently a friend of mine passed away. We had not seen each other for years but we grew up in the same neighborhood. It's my understanding from a reliable source that the wife of my friend died a few months before he died but he could not handle it. He literally never overcame her death. First, he received grief counselling but shortly afterwards was admitted into a mental facility where he passed away. The optimist in me says how flattering it must be to love someone so deeply that you cannot move on with your life after his/her passing. Is this an acceptable reaction to a loss? Not for me to say. This is a hard situation.

My spirituality mandates that we take time to mourn, cherish fond memories, get on with our purpose in life and trust we will be reunited with all of our loved ones in the afterlife. For me this is the ideal and healthy approach. This approach has the power to negate effects that unhealthy codependence has particularly in its capability of capitulating. We must prohibit any codependent behavior that prohibits us from flourishing in our full potential.

Neither should we allow codependence to fall upon things nor unhealthy substances. I smoked cigarettes, not the *funny* ones, as a teen. (Okay if I'm being truthful I experimented with the funny ones too at least once or twice in my life but like a president once said I did not inhale!) For now, let's stick with the topic of cigarette smoking. I thought it was so cool to hang out with friends that smoked because it made me feel as though I were a part of the in crowd. Thankfully, cigarettes were not a good fit for me and the doctors told me at age nineteen to give them up. I'd had a mild respiratory attack on the L while en route to my summer job, which was at a hospital. The staff doctor took X-rays and told me I'd be okay if I quit immediately. That was not a problem – I quit cold. Truthfully, I started back about six months later and the chest pains resumed; it was at this time I quit smoking for the rest of my life! Today, you couldn't pay me one-million US dollars to smoke!

An acquaintance of mine freely spoke about previous issues with crack cocaine. He's been clean for over ten years and perhaps it's safe to proclaim that's a chapter in his life that will permanently reside in history. I asked him what was so amazing about it. I shared with him that I'd dabbled with reefer but hated the feelings of paranoia while under the influence – I didn't and don't like feelings of not being in control of my faculties. I mostly dabbled to look cool in front of my friends who frequently accused me of being a goody goody two-shoe. Side Note: One can count the number of times I experimented during my teens using both hands, not that this justifies why I experimented, it was wrong on so many levels and I should not have succumbed to peer pressure. Smoking marijuana is currently legal in some U.S. states so at least I wouldn't go to jail if I'd became addicted to it. Nevertheless, it's my understanding that marijuana is not addictive. I don't know if it's addictive or not, I'm just glad I never took a liking to it.

My acquaintance said smoking crack was the equivalent to smoking a blunt to the fiftieth power – a feeling that was super amazing. He stated that as addictive as crack is nothing compares to one's first high using it and that the addiction comes because you chase that initial high, which is never to be found, but crack users believe that if you keep smoking it that initial feeling will return. The feel-good feeling never returns but the user becomes an addict. This was incredible to hear. He also stated that I was lucky that I didn't particularly enjoy marijuana because people that enjoy marijuana highs oftentimes graduate to something stronger and more addictive like he did.

He said he jeopardized everything including his professional job, relationships and freedom. Yes, he'd done jail time. Codependence ruined his life; yet I'm happy to report that today he's doing great. He has several well-paying jobs and has restored relationships with family and loved ones and he thanks God for delivering him.

I've encountered alcoholics too. Although cardiac failure was the official cause of death in 2014, my stepfather was an alcoholic and was hospitalized numerous times throughout my childhood but he didn't experience his first bypass surgery until about ten years after he gave up drinking. His last bout with alcohol that dissuaded him from ever drinking again was due to his experience with delirium tremens. It's my understanding from friends who are medical professionals that delirium tremens is an acute episode of hallucination that is usually caused by withdrawal from alcohol. Dad had a specific type of DT called tactile hallucination that occurs when a false perception of tactile sensory input creates a hallucinatory sensation of physical contact with an imaginary object. Please note the example in the illustration below that showcases the experience of one having an episode of delirium tremens.

This diagram illustrates how this girl feels as though there are spiders attacking her but the reality is that it is a figment of her imagination that resulted as she experienced an episode of DTs which could indeed happen due to the excessive intake of alcohol. Before you think it, yes, Jesus did turn water into wine at the wedding celebration; however, here's the thing: Jesus himself did not drink or become intoxicated by wine or any form of liquor; and, the Bible clearly tells us not to drink or do anything in **excess** or to the point where it has the capability to harm us. (KJV, John 1:1-11)

Consider this: while some believers might advocate for absolute abstinence from alcohol Scripture doesn't prohibit believers from drinking. Instead, Scripture condemns drunkenness or being a slave to wine, "And be not drunk with wine, wherein is excess; but be filled with the Spirit," Ephesians 5:18. We can agree or disagree. The bottom line is that substance abuse of any kind has the potential to age you. Aging is manifested in outward appearance and chronologically. Human organs indisputably can develop pancreatic issues due to excessive drinking, respiratory/emphysema issues due to smoking. Other issues could also arise and cause mental instability; or worse innocent family and loved ones can suffer incontrollable situations such as the death of a loved one with substance abuse problems or heaven forbid, divorce due to situations that got out of hand. It's true that in life the aging process is inevitable. However, why rush it; shouldn't it be our goal to age gracefully without aging prematurely? We mustn't use age as a deterrent that keeps us from our goals and neither should we age prematurely by inviting unhealthy participations of elements (drugs, alcohol) that can prohibit us from setting and reaching goals.

I possess a mentality that now says age is nothing but a number mostly because I permitted my age to determine who I was for way too long. I did things later in life than planned. I wanted to earn my college degree three years after graduating from high school, immediately followed by having a cushy dream job that paid a minimal of six figures. I'd meet my husband and start a family while young and have at least two boys and two girls. I would take off work for as long as necessary but my company would appreciate me so much that they would allow me to work from home at my discretion. My seven-bedroom house would include help from my two nannies – one would be for the girls and one for the boys. My husband would also be a successful doctor, lawyer, or Indian Chief. Life would be amazing. We'd go to church on Sundays and have brunch afterwards. We'd frequently allow are brilliant children to miss school in order to attend family vacations that took place during the school year – of course we would hire a licensed tutor so they would not fall behind in their school assignments. After all, it would be mandatory to hire educators that would travel with us since there would be a minimum of three vacations a year, four if you count the vacation where we would leave the children with family members and nannies. My life did not go down like this. Not even close!

My husband, Timothy, and I didn't have children until we'd been married for five years. We had boys back-to-back, no girls! We live in a modest house and at the time of this writing are empty nesters.

I returned to college when our sons were in grade school to complete my BA. The dream job did not happen. In 2009 I attended seminary and received my seminary MA in 2013. At one point there were three people from the Glen clan in college, which was not fun for my one income husband. Not to mention private school for his nephew who came to live with us in 2007 when his mother passed away. Thankfully I earned an academic scholarship and grants that covered the majority of my post-graduate tuition expenses; in fact, my husband did not have to pay any tuition for me my last year in seminary and the good news is that I didn't accrue any student loans to repay for my master's program.

The point is I watched many people have children, celebrate college graduations, get dream jobs, buy new homes and cars way before I experienced any of it. The worst part is how I felt as I witnessed other people getting blessed left and right. I wasn't getting any younger and thought I was too old to experience obtaining any of the things I most wanted. "When God when?" is what I frequently asked as I cried out to God in thought and prayer. I felt like a total loser. I just knew that a college degree would be a milestone in my life...or so I thought.

I truly was proud to receive my bachelors. It was also great that my children were old enough to understand and celebrate with me; yet I was in for a rude awakening. A college degree in 2002 did not hold the same weight it held 20 years before that. At least not for me it didn't. I knew better than to expect that six-figure income but I had no idea how difficult it would be to obtain a regular job I liked that paid well. The job market was tight! I dabbled in insurance for a while because I thought since I possess the gift of gab I would go far in a sales position, not!!! I've always been clumsy in the workforce but nothing was odder than me trying to sell life and health insurance. First, it took forever just to pass the State exam to become licensed. Next, cold calling was a trip as no one wanted to be bothered except for a few; and they seldom or never committed to buying a policy. I felt like a fish out of water and lay awake crying at night about everything I went through to better my situation but nothing concrete developed.

To this day I remind friends with great careers how blessed they are. Some call it luck, but whatever you want to call it it's great to earn an income doing something that you're passionate about. So many of us tolerate our jobs simply because they generate income. But blessed are those that have jobs/careers that pay well in addition to bringing fulfillment. I long to experience generating a professional salary doing something I'm totally passionate about. I work as a volunteer with the hopes of someday producing an impressive income. I've also gotten paid a modest salary for the work performed at one of my volunteer endeavors. How modest? It pays one of my lower bills, and no, not the cell phone, one lower than that. The point is I strongly believe the day will come when I reap the harvest of my labor. I better understand how to be a good steward over money. I also understand how I must financially bless others. We are not blessed to be selfish – we are blessed to be a blessing to others in need!

I also understand how blessed I am because of my husband. I've essentially been a stay at home mom since my youngest was three. We never planned for it to happen that way but life's circumstances mandated it. Staying at home was great at first but got old very quickly because I had to learn how to be satisfied with not shopping for shoes and clothes as much not to mention buying things for the house. I watched a lot of HGTV and frequently fantasize about how much fun it would be to totally update my house appliances and furniture. Over the years I've bought a few pieces here and there but always on a budget and cognizant about when items would be reduced to the sale price. It would be wonderful to shop without the concern of items being too expensive. I'm not saying that I'd require having custom made furniture (though that would also be nice); it would just be great to shop for exactly what I want without costs being an issue. I prefer quality stuff – not cheap stuff that may need to be replaced sooner rather than later.

Over the years I've learned how to be content and believe obsessing over things could inadvertently accelerate the aging process; or cloud one's judgment of what's really important in life. Now I count my blessings and appreciate what I have as opposed to bellyaching over what I don't have.

Another example is the car I drive. During the spring of 2011 we had a hailstorm in Chicago which totally damaged our already aged car. I guess we never repaired it mostly because the storm didn't cause damage to mechanical conditions – the car is just less attractive due to the golf ball sized dents sporadically dispersed over the hood overtly displaying the damage Mother

Nature did. I drive this car proudly dents and all! Call me weird but I've actually grown to like them because it's something humbling about driving a dented-up car. Don't misunderstand me; I'd welcome a new Lexus with open arms but until the Lord blesses me with one I shall be content to drive what gets me from Point A to Point B.

Driving a dented-up car has another advantage: do others judge me because of what I drive? Or accept me for who I am? Let's be honest, we Americans are known for loving our cars. We get accolades from neighbors when we drive new shiny cars and SUVs. Many consider one a success depending on what he or she drives. It doesn't matter that the Lexus owner might have bills up to wī-źū as long as he or she is driving in style they are automatically considered successful. It's true...that's the mentality in many circles.

When my mother was alive she drove a Mercedes Benz. It wasn't even new when she bought it but she got warm stares and heads turned wherever she went. I had the pleasure of driving it a couple of times, once to work and once to a party. It was before my husband and I had children. What I remember most is that I was an instant hit! People didn't care after I told them it was my mother's car all they saw was M-E-R-C-D-E-D-E-S!

Unfortunately, she let someone do some work on it and it was stolen and she never replaced it. Someone was envious. Envy isn't an excuse for stealing but I remember my mom's countenance after her *baby* was taken. She was devastated (but she eventually got over it). My takeaway from her sad experience is not to ever become so attached to something to the point where my spirit is forever crushed if it's ever taken from me. This doesn't mean I'm not sensitive to tragedies; it's just that I personally hope to overcome the loss of any material item, heaven forbid, if anyone steals from me. I'd be sad but would not want my entire countenance to be forever changed due to some unwelcomed violation. Hopefully I'd mourn the violation of something being stolen for a brief period of time and then move on with the expectation that things can always be replaced.

During my first semester in seminary I took a Spiritual Integration Lab that was a course requirement. These labs were a time of bonding with your SIL sisters and sharing about classes, life, spirituality, God, Jesus and whatever other topics arose. The instructor was nice and the students were welcoming. The question was asked: what would you do if you suddenly had to leave your home for whatever reason? It was the instructor's first semester too; she and her family uprooted from another state and moved to Chicago because of her husband's career.

I'd like to believe that as comfortable as I am in my home I could give it up if it ever became necessary; but inwardly I knew I would only want to give my home up for a bigger and better one. I was truthful and responded, "I'd be hard-pressed if I had to give up my house!" that was then; yet today this would still make me sad but for a different reason. I strongly desire to update my house to my total satisfaction so it would sadden me more if I were forced to leave it before I had the opportunity to remodel it. This is silly but it's the truth.

My prayer is that I'm not too attached to anything. It's not like I can carry *things* with me to the next realm after my transition from life as we know it. Therefore, we mustn't fret over things lest we age prematurely over materialism only to discover that we could indeed experience fulfillment without possessing too many things.

So age is nothing but a number. This is how I talked myself into returning to school. Oh make no mistake I made excuse after excuse not to finish and they were valid. I simply could not afford college tuition. We were a one income family and it just didn't seem fair to put that on my husband. This is when I decided to pray and ask God to make it happen. God made a way out of no way! I had been walking around with my lip on the floor when Tim (my husband) asked me what was wrong with me. I shared that I desperately wanted to return to school because I felt myself slipping into a place of not caring anymore. A long story shortened, we used the bulk of our tax returns that year to finance the balance I'd owe to my undergrad college. My foot was finally in the door and I was determined to finish. I had anxiety about being in a classroom full of youngsters but quickly overcame that. I've always loved my undergraduate alma mater, Columbia College Chicago. It was such an exciting and creative environment. I was so thirsty that I exceeded my best academic expectations. I graduated with honors and made straight A's my final semester. It was a great feeling that after years of being out of school I took the bull by the horns, so to speak, and was academically successful.

President Roosevelt quoted, "The only thing we have to fear is fear itself." I get that now so my advice to you is simply to go for it. Just do it! You can sit around dreaming about it while aging in the process or you can make every reason in the world to make it happen. Choose the latter. Franklin D. Roosevelt was up against unbelievable odds and could have made plenty of excuses – "I'm too old to do this" or "this is too hard" or "people are going to hate me because the country is in the worst depression ever…" Instead he kept it moving in grace and dignity. Matter of fact history buffs know that Franklin D. Roosevelt had campaigned against Herbert Hoover in the 1932 presidential election by saying as little as possible about what he might do if elected. Even in his closest working relationships, none of the president-elect's most intimate associates felt as if they knew him well. His wife Eleanor might be the exception. The easygoing, witty Roosevelt used his great personal charm to keep most people at a distance. In campaign speeches, he favored an optimistically gentle paternal tone sprinkled with humor. Interestingly enough his first inaugural address took on an unusually solemn, religious quality. Go figure. This turned out to work to his advantage due the fact that the 1933 depression had reached its peak. President Roosevelt's first inaugural address outlined in broad terms how he hoped to govern and reminded Americans that the nation's "common difficulties" concerned "only material things." Hmmm. Here we're reminded again about the ill effects of materialism spoken from one of America's historic presidents.

Therefore it's true: hashtag, age truly is nothing but a number. Whether or not one gets premature wrinkles due to being overly concerned with materialism is totally left up to the individual. I'm reminded of a Scripture in the Christian Bible regarding worry: "Therefore I say unto you, Take no thought for your life, what ye shall eat, or what ye shall drink; nor yet for your body, what ye shall put on. Is not the life more than meat, and the body than raiment? Behold the fowls of the air: for they sow not, neither do they reap, nor gather into barns; yet your heavenly Father feedeth them. Are ye not much better than they? Which of you by taking thought can add one cubit unto his stature? Therefore I tell you, do not worry about your life, what you will eat or drink; or about your body, what you will wear. Is not life more than food, and the body more than clothes? Look at the birds of the air; they do not sow or reap or store away in barns, and yet your heavenly Father feeds them. Are you not much more valuable than they? Can any one of you by worrying add a single hour to your life?" (KJV, Matthew 6:25-27)

No one can dispute the last line, which when translated in modern day English means, "can any of us extend our lives by worrying?" No we cannot! We can shorten our lives. Without any points of reference, we can agree that worry has the potential to cause headaches, hypertension, ulcers and the like. Many lose focus; some become depressed all which are due to the lack of control over that five-letter word spelled W-O-R-R-Y! Knock it off and stop doing this to yourself! Try a difference approach when anxiety of any type arrives at your doorsteps. If you must worry make it your last resorts. In other words, do everything humanly (and spiritually) possible before you submit to worrying about something that most likely is beyond your control anyway.

Again, I'm not insensitive to tragedy; but worry isn't the same as grieving or being upset over a life-threatening illness. What I'm offering is that worry will not help your situation; yet finding an alternate way off coping can be physiologically better for you.

With that said, new hashtag: #ImYoungandWorryFree!

# Chapter
## $\mathcal{S}ix$

## Job Stagnation

$\mathcal{M}$y initial thought was to dedicate this chapter only to people that have been in the workforce for at least five or ten years; who absolutely don't have any passion for their current job – they are indifferent about how they feel about their jobs and just tolerate it in order to earn a paycheck. They go through the motion of the daily routine out of habit as well as for survival. Yet this chapter is highly recommended to every adult who hates everything about their jobs. The manner in which they earn their living is a moot point because they positively unequivocally hate their job for whatever length of time they've invested working there. This chapter is also dedicated to you if you fit the bill somewhere in between these scenarios.

For example, you've only been in your current position for six months but you know it is not for you. You don't fit in, you hate your duties, you can't stand neither your boss nor coworkers and you lay awake at night wishing you didn't have a car note because between paying off the car and monthly rent/mortgage, there's no way you could quit your job due to the fact that you would no longer be able to support yourself. Furthermore, you would no longer be able to maintain your current lifestyle. Matter of fact, you don't actually care about lifestyle and would quit your job in a heartbeat if you could survive on the basic essentials for survival, that is, food, shelter and the clothes you already own. For a predetermined amount of time you'd gladly sacrifice shopping sprees, entertainment as well as frequent trips to Starbucks if it meant you could survive without going to that place five days a week that you absolutely abhor.

Solution: start planning your escape immediately! I happen to believe the saying, "if there's a will there's a way." I also believe you must strategize your move by mapping out a step-by-step plan in the direction you plan to go. The question is not whether or not you can leave that job you hate. The question is: when will you start planning your escape?!

Before I discuss ideas about how you can accomplish this I need to share my experience. My plan of action finally worked out for me but over a long period a time. Please, don't assume that since I have a husband it was *easy* for me. I had the moral support of my husband BUT my husband did not pay my bills when I quit my job to become a stay-at-home mom. It wasn't that he didn't want to; it was that back then he could not comfortably afford to pay the bills I had created. During the early days we had too many babysitting challenges and decided it was best if I quit my job in order to be with our children. It made sense because Tim earned more money than me; plus, he did not hate his job. Another factor for consideration is that my salary was modest – it seemed as though I was only working to pay the babysitter without much left over to contribute to household bills. I was an assistant for an advertising agency.

As I look back on those days I probably should have filed for bankruptcy. Eventually I worked for temp agencies and had many part-time jobs, which enabled me to work my schedule around my husband's schedule without the necessity of paying a babysitter.

It was fun at the beginning not to worry about the hustle and bustle of working, picking up the kids from daycare without rushing, getting dinner, taking long luxurious baths, watching an absurd amount TV and then repeat the process day in day out. Truthfully if I had those days to relive I would do things a lot differently. I would have taken the time to first identify my passions and talents and then move in the direction of them. Like many from my generation I was raised to believe that one must obtain a college degree in order to secure a good job, which usually consists of going to work for someone else. Working in corporate American was always awkward for me and I invested too many years working jobs that simply were not a good fit for me.

Also, I lacked focus and accumulated bills as I worked jobs I hated. Big mistake! It was unwise to accumulate debt due to purchasing material items that had to be paid for no matter how much I hated my job. But when you know better you do better (or should do better).

The point is to encourage you not make the mistake I made by investing too many years in a livelihood that makes you miserable. In case you've already invested too many years into a job/career that you're dissatisfied with I reiterate that it's not too late for you to change your circumstances. As I stated earlier you need a plan of action. Side Note: don't let your age stop you from making a change, be it a new job or whatever, treat yourself to some type of fulfillment that can permanently bring you out of your rut.

I worked for a well-known parcel delivery service as I planned to return to school to complete my bachelors. They had a program called "earn as you learn" that enabled employees to earn an income as they attended college. I will never understand why so many people I met seemed to hate it but did little or nothing to work toward seeking a better position. They were seasoned employers who could have easily been reimbursed for one-hundred percent of their tuition. I worked next to a lady in a section call *small sorts*. Newcomers like me received daily location assignments on the belt so it was not uncommon to work next to someone different every other day or so. She told me that she used to worked in their accounting department as a bookkeeper but got laid off which was how she ended up working in *small sorts*. I literally had only been there a couple of weeks when I applied for the tuition reimbursement program, which I eventually received. However, the office administrator at the hub where I worked did not submit my paper work to the corporate office that approved tuition reimbursements, which prohibited me from getting the full benefit but thankfully one of my immediate supervisors explained to me how not to entrust certain things to certain people without following up. That's another story for another book. I was able to receive some tuition reimbursement even if some of it had been detained.

One lady who worked next to me in small sorts was a talker and frequently struck up conversations regarding her work experience. I inquired as to why she hadn't returned to school. Her children were grown and gone, which meant she and her husband were empty nesters. She said she was too old to return to school. I didn't dare ask her age but my best guess is that she wasn't a day older than forty-five. I told her I was going back to school and encouraged her to return to school as well. I volunteered to bring literature about the school since it wasn't as common to do an Internet search for college curricula (this may have been during the transitional period between online catalogs versus mailing hard copies of college catalogs via U.S. mail if memory serves me correctly). The school I informed my coworker about has an accounting program and was listed in the company's directory to receive full reimbursement to all employees (unlike my school which at the time was only listed for partial reimbursement). It was convenient for me to pick up the college pamphlets since the school with the accounting program was geographically located near my undergraduate alma mater and both schools were not far from the hub where we worked. She giggled and said it was okay because she was too old and too tired to return to school. I shared with her how my mother returned to school later in life and opened her own business. I figured if she knew about someone else in her age group that had successfully returned to school she could likewise tackle the academic world and obtain a college degree, which would have enabled her to be eligible for a better position within the company (or at a different company if no adequate jobs were available).

Needless to say, she told me not to bring pamphlets. I had the nerve to be inwardly angry and believe me you from that point further I never listened to her complain about her job! I had (and probably still have) little patience for people that complain but do not take steps toward bettering their situations. I don't believe college is for everyone; I do believe however, that stagnation towards any goal is not an option! One does not have to go to college in order to better themselves – one must become knowledgeable about whatever field they desire to pursue if they expect to have any success. Nowadays it's very easy to self-educate on practically any area of interest.

Another lady, one of my supervisors, didn't complain about her job; instead she expressed how she wished she could earn more money. She was a single mom with two beautiful daughters in grade school. I don't recall her name but I had much respect for her and her work ethic. She expressed how she would study massage therapy in a heartbeat if she could but couldn't because her work schedule was too inflexible for her to sign up for classes. At that time the parcel company did not honor online courses for their tuition reimbursement program so even if an online program existed for massage therapy my supervisor would have had to pay the tuition out-of-pocket.

She expressed how lucky I was to have a husband that supported me. Of course being the smart mouth I used to be I retorted that the grass is always greener on the other side. (I probably was angry with Tim for something at the time.) My response to her was that while I'm grateful for my husband he might trade me in at any time for a younger model. Trust me, I'm not and wasn't insecure – it's just that my "be cautious for nothing" nature had influenced my mindset. I always hope for the best but never assume anything.

My suggestion to her was since she'd been with the company a while she should request specific hours that didn't interfere with her school schedule. I shared with her about how she qualified for grants and that she should at least start off taking one course. *Small sorts* had weekends off and she could have possibly taken a Saturday class. I took my kids to class with me whenever I couldn't get a sitter; sure I got flack but I did what it took since my husband had to work and we couldn't afford a reliable babysitter (both of our mothers had passed away by this time). I would have offered to babysit if she decided to return to school. And of course I would not have charged her.

Unfortunately, she didn't feel it was doable and did not enroll. Although we've lost touch over the years I wonder if she ever dared to chase her dreams. She was smart and decent and my prayer for her, wherever she may be, is that she and her girls are doing well.

My mother returned to school late in life and eventually found her niche. I was in the eighth grade when she received her degree in business administration. She opened up a traveling agency after she spent too many years in corporate America being passed over for jobs she was qualified to do. I don't know how the world of travel business worked during the early 1990's but my mother received a big contract from the City just before she got sick then later died of cancer. Her dream came true! Her dream would not have come true if all she did was talk about how dissatisfied she was with her career path as opposed to planning her escape toward a career that impassioned her. Mama was in her fifties when she started her own traveling agency and I believe that if she could do it so can you!

Ready? Let's go!!!

There are three basics you must take care of as you plan your strategy of escape: (1) change your mindset, (2) be willing to make sacrifices; and (3) know exactly what it is that you want or at least have a keen idea of what you want. Please Note: As with anything there are no guarantees in life; however, there are actions you must take if you are serious about getting out of your job rut.

The plan of action starts with your mindset! It doesn't matter if you're on this side of forty or that side of forty you have the ability to start a new job, if that's what you want, or you can continue to be miserable and stuck. The first thing you must do is change the way you think. I'm no expert I'm only sharing with you how things changed for others and for me when we decided to redirect our mindsets. Forget the mindset that says "possible but not probable." Instead tell your mind that what seems to be an improbability will definitely become a probability. You will accomplish your goal and surely you must be determined to enjoy the journey while in route.

For years I wanted to return to college to complete my BA and made many reasons why it could not be done. It wasn't until I told myself that one way or another I'm going to get my degree that it actually came into fruition. Today I hold two degrees – BA and MA. The first hurdle I had to jump was the hindrances of my mind. And, I'm going to let you in on a secret. Although I'm proud of myself for earning two college degrees I did not need either degree to accomplish my career goals. Please don't misunderstand me: my master's program was so intense that it actually ignited the discipline I need to write. Plus, I'm confident my degrees will come in handy if I ever decide to seek a traditional career…yes even at my current age.

This also shouldn't discount anyone from earning college degrees because truthfully, having a degree does make you more marketable not to mention how possessing a college degree is also required for many professions such as educators/professors, doctors and attorneys, to name a few. A degree informs potential employers that you know how to think and/or are committed to being teachable.

It was challenging for me to reprogram my mind to accept the fact that learning after being away from school for so many years was doable. I did not understand before I returned to school that understanding my purpose through my passion was crucial; and in my opinion, that's the one thing that college does not teach (unless something's changed in recent years).

Money was tight but I decided that I would return to school. I didn't know how but I knew that within three months from the time I decided to return it was going to happen. I communicated with the Bursar's Office to establish my tuition balance from previous semesters, what or if transcripts from previous schools were needed for re-enrollment and most of all what grants/scholarships were available. I spent a lot of time praying and meditating. I told God how important this was and asked him to help me. I'd like to believe it was God that softened my husband's heart because that year the bulk of our income tax returns went to paying off the previous balance.

There was still one more problem: how would I pay for the current semester even if the past debt was settled? Enter the parcel delivery service tuition reimbursement program where I worked. They offered a tuition incentive program and that is how I financed my undergraduate tuition in addition to one student loan I took out. In fact, it grieved me to take out a student loan but the good news is that I only took out one loan mostly because I watched my husband pay off his loans that seemed to take an eternity to repay. The difference is that he took out loans every academic year whereas I only took out one loan.

Instead of making excuses not to return to school I made reasons to return and finish my program. Not only did I complete my program but I completed another post-graduate program called "Semester in LA" where select students got to study an accelerated program on the CBS Lot in Studio City, California. It was most exciting! We had to present our projects to industry professionals at the end of the program and I am grateful for the experience.

The way I see it is that I could have wallowed and whined in self-pity about how could I finish college; or I could have been determined to return and finish. I chose the latter and it started with what I told my brain, which was the reverse of my previous negative mindset that got me nowhere fast.

Another friend of mine also wanted to return to school and like me, she didn't think she could afford it. I encouraged her to start making small payments toward her past due tuition payments until she could figure it out. She started out making twenty-dollar payments that quickly escalated to one hundred-dollar payments. This bill ultimately got paid off and before she knew it she was back in school with the goal of completing her masters. I'd reminded her to check with her company for tuition incentives. She initially said it was no use because the company (an ad agency) was suffering financially and *probably* couldn't afford its tuition reimbursement program. I insisted she had nothing to lose by checking. Her company paid for 90% of her master's program!

See oftentimes we tell ourselves no when in fact the answer is already yes! Change the way you think. There truly is something about the power of positivity. Furthermore, you don't always have to know in advanced how things will work out – you must assume in your mind beforehand that they will just somehow work out favorably.

The second point is we must be willing to make sacrifices. I did not immediately quit my job at my husband's first suggestion. It was August of 1993 when he asked me to quit and I wanted to quit on the spot but I hesitated because I knew that if I quit I would instantly become totally financially dependent on my husband for everything and that would be an adjustment. I quit at the beginning of the following New Year, January 1994. Later, spring of 1994, I went to work for a temp agency and received a long-term assignment at a major bank that offered me a fulltime job that I refused because although I enjoyed the people and did a good job I knew in my heart of hearts that working as an administrative assistant was not a good fit for me. To my surprise the manager at the bank where I temped agreed to the obnoxious salary I'd requested. I inwardly thought that he would turn down my salary request; it was then that I knew I'd done a good job because I had never before made that much money (thirty-five thousand a went a long way back in 1994 especially for someone like me who hadn't yet earned a college degree nor was I skilled in a trade besides being a mediocre typist).

This was one of the sacrifices I made to be a stay-at-home mom and although I did not immediately return to school there was definitely a huge mental weight lifted since I no longer had to go to a job that was not the best fit for me.

This sacrifice prepared me for more necessary future sacrifices that enabled me to complete both undergrad and grad school. I didn't have the luxury of shopping sprees but there was a security that came with being there to raise our children without the dependence of childcare outside the home.

Your sacrifice may be something totally different. Locate what sacrifices may be needed in order to help you reach the goal of making job stagnation a thing of your past!

Lastly, it is not enough to know that you hate your current job or predicament. You must know what it is you would be doing if you did not have to do what it is that you hate but need for survival. Many don't know this but knowing what it is that excites you is half or for sure a third of the way towards getting you closer to your goal. And, in case you don't know for sure what it is that you want to do consider this: what is the one thing that excites you? What legal thing would you be doing if you could generate an income from performing it?

Don't consider me self-indulgent but again I'll use myself as an example since I know my own story better than I know anyone else's. I love to talk and have the gift of gab. I use to be in sales and was a State licensed insurance agent for life and health except nowadays they're called insurance producers, at least in Illinois. I thought I'd be successful at this since I enjoy talking. Not so much though; sure, I enjoy socializing but I learned the hard way there is so much more to sales than just talking. Needless to say, after dabbling in insurance for a couple of years I quit and let my license lapse. A friend of mine begged me to keep my license current but I knew in the depths of my being that that career simply was not a good fit. So, I moved on!

Theology and philosophy are two of my favorite topics. I love to talk and I love theology. I am a minister. Who knew? LOL. I enjoy praying for and with people. I enjoy learning about all types of denominations and most importantly I believe in God, or if you prefer, a Supreme Being. Furthermore, ministry work is a field where work is always available if by no other method than volunteering in local churches and parachurches. I may not earn a six-figure income and that's okay because I love what I do! I enjoy interacting and praying with and for people. I also enjoy the volunteer work outside my church.

About three years ago I volunteered to be a volunteer bell-ringer for the Salvation Army. It was my first experience as a bell-ringer and I loved it! I didn't care about the Chicago wind that seemed to rip through me on that cold winter day because the people I encountered were wonderful (even though some did not drop money into the kettle. It's okay, I've prayed for them and they'll give more generously next time...hopefully).

I enjoy helping and encouraging people – it's my God-given purpose to encourage others. I haven't always understood this but as I stated earlier, "When we know better we should do better." I'd be the first to admit that I don't have all the answers; but I have a lot of life experience and am always willing to share info that has the capability of enriching the life of another; or inspiring others to become their best selves and find contentment in life.

Another pastime I have always enjoyed is writing because for me it's therapeutic. I don't purport to be a Jane Austen though Sister Margaret Ann, my sophomore literature teacher, said I was an excellent writer and that I should "Keep it up." No one until then had ever said anything praiseworthy about my creative writings. I wished I had had the courage and discipline to develop as a writer at that point in my life. I don't regret it...I only wonder "what if?"

Fast-forward to the present, I'm satisfied if I can inspire others to view life through a different more positive lens. Especially for those that are challenged about viewing the glass as being half-full. I feel as though one of my goals is met if an individual at least considers looking at things from a more positive perspective after he or she has engaged in a conversation with me or after viewing something I've written that's inspirational. Yet if nothing optimistic comes into manifestation and if heaven forbid I somehow wasn't able instill positivity into the life of another, I still feel victorious because no matter the outcome my objectives are always pure. For me it's a win-win situation especially considering how deliberate and positive my intentions undeniably are. I say this to demonstrate that I'm determined to practice what I preach by viewing the glass as being half-full.

People frequently wonder about their purpose in life; there are many books written on the subject. We don't have to over analyze it. Our purpose is almost always centered around something that comes natural to us and/or something that excites us. It's that simple! You know better than anyone what excites you. So as a familiar cliché suggests, "Just Do It!"

My youngest son was a theatre major who attended one of the country's top universities. The issue is that he's always hated general studies but he enjoys entertaining – acting, dancing, singing – the whole kitten caboodle. He desperately desires to earn a living as a performer and understands his area of interest is extremely competitive (but what isn't competitive these days?). My advice to him is to perform and act in front of us (his family) now. To my surprise he listened and routinely performs monologues for his dad and me and we love it! It gives us the chance to encourage him as well as affords him the opportunity to keep his thespian skills fresh and he's less mopey about when his big break will happen. I accredit his love for the arts and performing as the source of his joy.

So you see, you can do whatever you like way before you earn a salary from it. There's a quote that goes something like, "find something you enjoy doing and you'll never have to work again." I don't know who said this but I'd love to shake her/his hand. We put way too much focus on money and make no mistake I know we need finances to survive; yet we also need peace of mind to survive because without peace of mind you won't be able to enjoy any amount of money.

You may find that if you start doing things you enjoy it might enable you to work that job you hate with less hostility towards it. View the job you hate as a stepping stone toward the future career that you're passionate about, your dream job. You may surprise yourself and discover that you can indeed hang on until you've completed your exit strategy.

What's the step-by-step strategy? It is the strategy that you make for yourself after you incorporate the three aforementioned basics, which are (1) change your mindset by becoming inwardly positive even when you struggle to be positive; (2) be willing to make sacrifices; and, (3) know what excites you. I believe it's *un*necessary to inundate you with some esoteric chart that starts small and builds to some obnoxious overstated psychological so called foolproof intellectual methodical technique that will instantly improve your life! Instead it's critical to get you to think for yourself. Charts, while impressive and aesthetically pleasing to the eye, don't necessarily reflect what each individual need as a personal instructional guide, which is why I recommend that you first incorporate the three basics – positive mindset, sacrifice and know what you're passionate about; then proceed to follow your own instincts, which usually never fail if followed in clarity. Many, including myself, used age as an excuse to remain stagnated; yet this simple formula worked for me as well as other friends and associates I've met during my life's journey.

With that said, discover your dream career and what you like and simply go for it!

# Seven

## Adults vs. Youngsters

This is the fish-out-of-water, so to speak, chapter and while it is mostly directed toward adults that encounter preteen and teens; preteens, teens as well as adults can benefit from its contents. Whether adults that have their own children or come in contact with youth via their careers (teacher, counselors, clergy, coach), or however else there may be a connection to this age group, consider the possibility that even if you are on either side of forty you are never too old to learn from individuals who happen to be younger than you. It never ceases to amaze me whenever I witness adults who are consistently impatient with children and frequently sigh if the child doesn't accomplish a task in the manner the adult would have accomplished that same task. Forget the fact that the minor has fewer years on the planet and less experience in life in general.

I was about ten years old when I waited for a friend of mine to get permission to hang out with me at my house. She was ten and her sister was twelve. Their mother never took the time to teach them to cook; instead she'd yell their heads off if the roast and side dish were not cooked to perfection. I've witnessed similarities in lack of patience in adults from various families as far back as I can remember until this day. Although I am now a full-grown adult I simply don't understand how it is that our grown-up expectations of kids are frequently displayed. It's ridiculous and unrealistic. We expect kids to respect us no matter how unruly we communicate to our children. Yet if that same kid spoke to us in the same adult tone, we'd be ready to "tap that ass" for being disrespectful! I'm talking about corporal punishment through a whipping/spanking of chastisement, forgetting that children learn by example more so than by doing what we tell them to do. Respect should be a two-way street at any age.

I believe in teaching a child instead of being too quick to strike them. Many new age parents share this belief. Nevertheless, believers may quickly quote the passage in the Bible that says something to the effect that if you don't spank your kids you don't love them (Proverbs 13:24). I absolutely agree with this Scripture; yet I maintain that young children should first be taught proper behavior as opposed to being spanked. Adults should be smart enough to revise a plan which encourages children to obey. No child under six should be spanked in my opinion because these are the explorative years and they're still learning. Besides, more often than not parents should never spank or hit a child while angry. Parents should calm down before disciplining. This doesn't mean that if a child tries to burn down the house they shouldn't immediately be disciplined. This means that parents may be more affective if they first calm down and discipline in love.

Children seven years and older have better understanding of rules so the rod should not be spared if they do something obnoxious or deserving of a punishment. Talking with children beforehand and explaining why they must be punished corporally should precede the act because this shows the child your concern and love for them. Perhaps they will think twice before committing that infraction again.

My confession is that I have had to apologize to my own sons when they were younger for having too great an expectation from them and not always being as patient with them as I should have been. Like it or not, we frequently pass down residual parenting skills. I'm proud to admit that you can count the times on one hand that I felt the need to physically punish our sons throughout their entire childhood. During those times that I didn't spare the rod was because I felt as though they were grossly misbehaving and taking advantage of my niceness, which is why I felt compelled to show them who the boss actually was! Boundaries must be set with children.

It was a culture shock to me when the mom of a friend of mine from a different culture than me took the time to teach her how to complete certain tasks. We were barely in our teens when I observed how gentle her mother was and how she explained the significance of sweeping before mopping to prevent the mop from getting overly clunky and run the risk of scratching the floors as oppose to getting them clean. Common sense suggests that sweeping automatically comes before mopping. What shocked me was how her mom took time to explain the importance of the order of those tasks. In another instance, she explained to her daughter how she should pour the grease off the chops before she added water to smother them in order to make gravy. Her mother taught how unhealthy most cooking grease is and how they must do to their best to drain the frying pan of oil. I would stare in amazement because even though I was taught some things it wasn't in the same manner as I'd witnessed in my friend. My great-grandmother taught me a lot about cooking and she was definitely gentle and patient. Unfortunately, she passed away before my cooking skills were fully developed. This isn't to disrespect my parents because they worked fulltime and usually cooked the heavy stuff after work. They seldom asked me to cook and told me to just focus on my homework; but I recall being criticized by the time I was a high school senior for not being interested in learning how to cook.

Switching gears, too often we adults believe we can't learn from youngsters because we surpass them in life experience since we are years older. It's true we have the advanced age as well as the experience nevertheless this doesn't mean we can't learn from our youth sometimes.

I recall an episode of a cartoon that aired during the mid-1990s called, *Bobby's World*, when Bobby's mother is tasked with making cupcakes for her preschooler's class. She panics because she runs out of green food coloring to make the green colored icing in correlation to the specified color theme. The mother overdramatizes the dilemma because she doesn't have time to wait for the father to get home from work so she could run to the grocery store to get exactly what she needs. Bobby, her preschool aged son, tugs at her apron as he tries to tell her not to worry but of course she's sick with worry lest she becomes the laughing stock as opposed to the perfect mom who makes perfect food for all events. This could ruin her reputation! Sick with anguish she finally bends down to listen to Bobby, who tells her what he learned in school that day. He tells her that if she mixes the yellow and blue colors together she would indeed get the green color that she desires. The mother becomes overjoyed and smooshes the kid with kisses galore. The four-year-old feels smart because this one act he learned in school yielded much love and extra attention from his mother. It's a win-win for both.

If the mother had immediately listened to her son in this scenario she would have saved herself some grief. Food color is not a life-threatening ordeal in real life. The point is that in real life it is actually okay to hear youngsters out by listening to them sometimes. This doesn't mean we must always do what they tell us; instead it means that we must respect them by hearing their views and opinions. We demand respect from them and we should also render respect to them in return.

Many adults, especially those of us that are thirty-five and older, were raised and taught to do what we were told without question. My generation was expected to do what our parents told us to do in addition to what our adult neighbors told us to do. In fact, if our parents received a negative report from neighbors and heaven forbid our teachers, we had serious consequences to deal with as a result of being disobedient or disrespectful. This may still be the case in some circles but nowadays it seems youth have the "You're not my mama/daddy…you can't tell me what to do!" attitude.

I don't know if it's due to the fact that many adults have lost the respect of youngsters (for whatever reason) or if it's because today's youth are intrinsically rebellious, or perhaps it's combination of both, in either case being older does not automatically mean that the elder is always right. It's imperative to cite that this is not an inducement for pre-teens and teens to challenge or be disrespectful to their elders in any way. Therefore teens, before those consequential notions begin SQUASH the thoughts of mouthing off and displaying bad attitudes. You have no right to be disrespectful! There may be times when circumstances are unfair and your teacher or whoever has authority over you might be unfair to you; even if this is the case, don't take matters into your own hands (this statement assumes you are not in a life-threatening situation).

The best way to deal with unfairness is to report it to the proper authorities. If you have an unfair teacher ask your parents to schedule an appointment with the principal in an attempt to solve the problem. Everybody has a boss or someone to hold them accountable for their actions.

Think about it. What good will it do you to cuss out a teacher who has the final say in whether or not you will graduate in your senior year? Or pass to the next level from whatever grade you're in currently. You must ask yourself if it's worth it to allow that teacher to stop you from getting your diploma. I'm sure you've heard it a thousand times from teachers or maybe even a parent, "I've already got mine but you still have to get yours..." so don't be stuck on stupid! Handle your business in an acceptable and intelligent manner. Not only will you be the better person for it – you will also display great character-development and maturity.

A real live experience comes to mind. I had a conversation with an undergraduate professor who handpicked students to travel to Princeton University to attend and participate in a science symposium. I was amongst the younger students in this selection and was definitely the only student that was married with children. She and I got to know each other better and swapped stories on the plane. She was of Middle East descent and smart as a whip! Somehow or another we starting talking about stereotypes of various races and how common it is that people typically show distrust of African-Americans especially teen men and young adult men.

She went on to say how her sons told her not to trust these teens that were not African- American but were another minority group that I won't cite here except to say there were foreigners. The specific details regarding the type of science program she'd previously been involved with are foggy but from my memory about the negative racial accusations are in the forefront of my memory bank. From what I recall there were a panel of staffers, including my professor, who were assigned with choosing minority students to participate in the science program that offered a modest income for need-based students. She and the *recruiters* left all the teens unattended to deliberate a few minutes before they made the decision as to which group would be awarded the opportunity. Money was stolen from the room the students were left unattended. One *recruiter* of the team *assumed* it was the African-American teens that stole the money when in reality the black teens had not stolen anything.

My professor learned after a full on investigation that it was not the black teens that had stolen from the professional; instead it was a different group of teens that had a reputation of being thieves. My professor's son had pre-warned her about the group that were thieves, which was why she was relieved she did not have the sole decision as to which group of youths got hired. Her primary purpose for being involved was to expound on academic/scientific expectations for the potential new hires. The professor was glad that she listened to her son and admitted that in the end she was glad that she didn't have the final decisions about which groups were hired. Also, it might have been possible for her to incorrectly judge the black students especially considering how innocent the group looked but were actually guilty.

Here the reality is that as brilliant as my professor is it took listening to someone younger, in this case her adult aged son, that reminded her to remain neutral about a group of people regardless of whatever normal preconceptions are regarding youths solely based on their race – especially considering how influential she was by having the power to express her opinions regarding who should be hired. It's so easy for us to jump on the bandwagon of another's prejudices without weighing situations for ourselves. I believe with all certainty that my professor would have acted in integrity even if her son had not forewarned her. However, sometimes extreme busyness causes us to delegate responsibilities without us being aware of every detail that was considered before final decisions are made.

Moreover, we may agree that sometimes it's the younger generation that has more tolerance regarding race relations. This may not always be the case but the optimist in me says and believes diversity is on the rise. Diversity can also be viewed in terms of incorporating a younger and perhaps fresher approach that alleviates stereotypical behaviors with respect to the wisdom that should accompany age.

Parents, another thing that bugs me is when you try to live your life vicariously through your child by demanding the child chooses to pursue a career or activity that is not a good fit for the child; or maybe she simply isn't interested and prefers to pursue her own area of interest.

What immediately comes to mind is when my youngest son was in high school. I participated in the Parent-Teacher board, commonly referred to as PTA, when I met many of my son's friends. All of his friends were nice, respectful and enjoyed interacting with me. It's not uncommon for talks of college choices to start in the eleventh grade during the times when students and parents alike are bursting with anticipation about the next chapter of the high schooler's life.

One of his friends expressed to me her love of art design and how she wanted to major in graphic design when she went away to college. The spark in her expression was priceless as she shared with me some of her drawings and talked about some of the technical ins and outs of computer animation. Our conversation actually helped me to envision what she spoke of when I took my son to a college tour to Academy of Arts University in San Francisco later that same schoolyear. I was impressed by how much she knew considering she had not yet visited any perspective colleges.

Later that same day I hung around campus to attend the PTA meeting. Her father was an active parent and kept up with the goings on at the school and was oftentimes outspoken during meetings. The parents, including me, respected him because of his involvement because usually it's assumed that female parents are expected to tend to school affairs more so than fathers. (Maybe that stereotype has/is changed/changing.) We usually socialized before the meeting and the atmosphere was always pleasant. The father of this young student asked me where was my son going to college and what would be his major. I told him we were visiting various colleges and that my son's major would be acting/theatre/dance with a minor in fashion design.

His expression turned fifty shades of red and he countered how difficult it would be for my son to establish a secure career in such competitive fields. I shared with him that my husband and I attended a college known for arts and how we understand the significance of following your passions. He countered and said passions don't pay the bills.

I inwardly started boiling because I felt his opinion was negative and unsolicited. The plan he mapped out for his daughter was his business. The plan we permitted with our children was our business. Both plans would yield a college education.

My following statement directed to him was how his daughter had shared with me her love for the arts and how knowledgeable and articulate she was about graphic design. By this time the nosy students entered the room because the

PTA occasionally gave them a chance to voice concerns about school business in predetermined meetings. Her father said in the presence of everyone that he was not going to pay for her to major in anything graphic or art; and that she was going to major in nursing because she would be guaranteed a job anywhere in the country with nursing credentials. She sat next to him and across from me which means I saw her face drop with sadness. Her expression deflated like a balloon. I asked her father what if she didn't want to be a nurse and also what if she went far in a career that she was actually interested in, but he insisted that it was ridiculous and that since she needed his financial support she had to major in the field he selected for her. I wanted to cry for her. I told him that my parents forced nursing on me too but before I could continue my spiel the meeting was called to order. I know his intentions were practical; yet he seemed to value misery overs practicality.

My mother, God rest her soul, desperately wanted me to attend nursing school so much so that she insisted that I become a candy striper at one of Chicago's prestigious hospitals. I told my mother that I struggled in science classes (especially during my high school years) and how much I hated anything science and that one must pass science related courses with A's in order to be successful in any medical field. She didn't listen and I became a candy striper. I enjoyed meeting people and the attention received as a result of "knowing so early in life" what I wanted to be. I wanted to make my mother happy but deeply resented her for forcing me into that program and then later to nursing school – another top program in the country.

I thought to myself that I should not worry because I knew I wouldn't score high enough on the ACT/SAT college test to be accepted into such a reputable school especially considering I went to prom with a guy friend the night before the test. The prom was on a Friday and the college entrance exam was early the next morning – there was no way I'd get accepted into such reputable university! Or so I thought…

I took the exam and actually tried to do well on it. I don't recall my numbers except to say they were low. My mother was relentless and told me to get some favorable recommendations from the nuns of the high school I attended. Damn! It worked. Sister Margaret Ann gave me a beautiful recommendation. She talked about how compassionate a person I am and how much of an asset to the medical profession I would be if given the opportunity. The principal also stamped her seal of approval in validation of how much character I possess. Double damn! I got accepted. The silver lining is that although the school is located in the city, my parents insisted that I move on campus and not work. They picked up all of my expenses. I suspect my grandmother pitched in financially as well because my mother had insisted that I give her a tour of my dorm room and campus.

As fate would have it, I had to drop an anatomy lab in my second semester because I was highly allergic to the formaldehyde. I also learned that I was extremely squeamish at the sight of blood! I begged my mother to let me go to another college that had a special program for social workers. People, from that time to the present, always feel comfortable about sharing personal details about their lives with me. I believed I would have made an excellent social worker, counselor or therapist. I never knew why my mother pushed so hard until after her death. A reliable family member told me that she had in fact been a candy striper and decided to get married right after high school. My older brother was a honeymoon baby and my mother essentially became a stay at home mom until after I was born. Needless to say, I dropped out of the nursing program way before I got to the practical portion of the training.

I neither blame the PTA father from my youngest son's high school, nor my mother, for desiring what they felt was best for their children. Also, being a parent of two college-aged sons I truly understand that it comes from a place of love. Speaking of our sons, one down and one to go! My oldest graduated from Occidental College in Los Angeles. I guess it's a matter of perspective but from the time our sons were old enough to talk I told them that they could major in anything they were interested in as long as they went to college (and even that assumes they are college material). When they became older I told them to let me know if college was not a good fit and we could figure something else out because I don't believe college is for everyone BUT I believe everyone must have a plan whether or not they attend college.

God respects people and according to the Christian Bible he is known to have occasionally changed his mind. God answers a specific prayer of one of his Old Testament kings on a deeply personal level. Wouldn't it be great if human parents would change their minds for the betterment of their children as opposed to being closed minded? Especially when it comes to career choices. God Almighty respects work ethic and my observation is how many biblical characters as well as current day people go far due to their possession of excellent focus and work ethic; and Hezekiah, the OT king who had excellent work ethic proves this.

Hezekiah became ill and was at the end of life when he besought God through prayer, lamented about how good of a servant he had been and asked God to increase the years of his life. God heard and answered Hezekiah's prayer, "…I have heard your prayer and seen your tears; I will heal you…**I will add fifteen years to your life**…'Prepare a poultice of figs.' They

did so and applied it to the boil, and he [Hezekiah] recovered"
2 Kings 20:5-7, KJV).

Christians consider God to be their spiritual father just as
many of us are fathers (or parents) here in the natural realm.
Assuming this is true, that is, God is our father; if he listens to us
who are we not to listen to youth? After all isn't God considered
the Ancient of Days? He's been around since forever and is
older than creation itself, which means if he can listen to us
then we can certainly listen to those who are younger than us.

Listening can save us from grief. Grief has the ability to age
us prematurely. We know aging is inevitable yet don't most of
us prefer to age gracefully? So why not consider that someone
besides us, including youngsters, may help alleviate premature
aging. Besides, the Bible gives this caveat: "Be anxious for
nothing, but in everything by prayer and supplication, with
thanksgiving, let your requests be made known to God"
(Philippians 4:6).

Okay young people I've thrown you a bone, so to speak,
therefore while I have your attention please follow me and give
special attention to the next chapter. I love young people and
while you frequently get a bad rap I feel to an extent that adults
paved the way to where many youngsters land in life be it a good
place or a less than desirable place.

# PART II

## It's A Young World After All

# Chapter

# *Eight*

## Let Me Holla at the Young People

*Y*oung people, you know I love y'all and what I'm about to say will come off as rude, abrasive and condescending; BUT I only ask that you hear me out and read the entire chapter before you make your final judgment regarding what I'm about to share. Fair deal? Okay, here we go!

Listen! I've got to say it: You don't know every dang thing! Many of you are intelligent and do extremely well academically for which I am proud of you. Those of you that are focused and respectful deserve accolades and let me congratulate you for a job well done! Please keep up the good work.

Yet and still, those of you who are smart must not equate being smart with knowing everything; neither should you become arrogant due to the gift of intelligence that you possess because as smart as you may be, you simply do not know everything! Some of you haven't been in the world two decades yet you think you know it all when in fact you don't know nearly as much as you think! Except maybe to be indignant with authority and constantly buck the tide. If this is you, STOP! Yeah, my tone is quite emphatic because hopefully this indignant tone will get your attention and also because it needs to be said.

I'm proud of those of you that happen to be sensible and respect authority. Let's face it, even the best of the best struggle with authority at some time or another but for those of you who continually avoid trouble and keep your misadventures with authority to a minimal, you deserve a shout-out so again, keep up the good work! Trust me, I know no one is perfect and everybody makes mistakes. We should learn from mistakes and strive to do better for ourselves and our loved ones.

Those of you twenty-one and under that habitually disrespect authority should consider the following scenarios before you travel down a path that leads to the point of no return. Maybe these real live circumstances will change your perspective in case you are too stubborn to rethink how you handle your business.

The names of the following true events have been changed to protect the not so innocent. Twinkles, a nineteen-year-old administrative assistant that still lives at home with her parents befriends thirty-four-year old Freckles, who works at the same company in a different department. Both ladies were good at their jobs and decided to meet in-person since they'd had numerous telephone conversations through scheduling meetings for their department heads. There was a fifteen-year gap in their ages but they became fast friends. Freckles asked Twinkles what did she do for fun on weekends and stated that she wanted to do something fun for a change since she and her husband were newly divorced. Twinkles told her about a neighborhood nightclub she'd heard about but never actually gone. Twinkles was flattered that someone fifteen years her senior felt she was cool enough to hang out with and decided they could hangout on that following Saturday assuming Freckles would secure a babysitter for her seventeen and fifteen-year-old children. Freckles said they were old enough to not require a babysitter but they indeed required adult supervision whenever she needed to be away from home more than a couple of hours especially at night time. Twinkles didn't care and was glad she didn't have to drive especially since her car was on its last leg. Twinkles was also grateful for whatever arrangements Freckles had to make in order for them to establish a friendship outside of work.

Twinkles warned Freckles as she got in her car that the club was located on a pretty rough side of town but they would be okay once inside. Freckles didn't care – just to have time outside of work and kids was music to her ears mostly because she'd been depressed over the divorce.

The club was rocking and neither lady could catch their breath before they were back on the dance floor with a new dance partner. Some of Twinkles club hopping friends also showed up and teased her about going to a club in the "hood." They knew she preferred upscale clubs that had a reputation of being sophisticated – clubs where you put on your coolest, classiest outfits. Twinkles retorted to her friends that fun is fun regardless of the location of the venue. She was proficient in not allowing others to kill her good mood.

The night was festive and they ended up staying until the club kicked them out. Two young guys, one about twenty-two and the other about twenty-seven asked Twinkles and Freckles where they lived and if they could hitch a ride. Twinkles rode with Freckles and this meant it was left up to Freckles to give the guys a ride; yet Twinkles felt suspicious about the older of the two. She excused herself and asked Freckles to join her as she went to the Lady's Room because she wanted to talk in private. Once there she told Freckles that although the guys seemed nice she didn't feel comfortable about giving people they'd just met a ride. She stated that the twenty-two-year-old seemed harmless but that her "spider" senses warned her against the other guy. Freckles insisted that both guys seemed harmless and that if it were her son that needed a ride she would be grateful if a stranger gave him a ride instead of him needing to rely on public transportation in such a horrible neighborhood. Twinkles fervently disagreed and told her okay but that she should at least take her home last no matter where the guys lived. Freckles said okay but she didn't hold to this.

Twinkles had hoped the guys would have left since it took them a long time to finish talking in the bathroom but no such luck. Freckles asked where they lived and decided she would drop the twenty-two year-old off first, then her buddy Twinkles and then the twenty-seven year-old guy would be dropped off last. Twinkles interrupted her and said, "Don't you mean you'll drop me off last?" but Freckles insisted that it would be going out of her way and route if she dropped Twinkles off last. The twenty-seven year-old was also insistent and asserted that it would be more convenient for her to drop him off last. The hairs on the back of Twinkles neck stood up because his insistence sealed how she inwardly felt about him. She knew her suspicions had not been a case of paranoia and demanded that Freckles take her home last. Freckles did not honor her request...after all she was the *older* of the two.

Once inside Twinkles kicked off her shoes and rubbed her aching feet. She was grateful she arrived home before her parents because she knew they would have given her flack about coming home so late at about three A.M. She knew her parents had their own party to attend not that they were party animals, quite the contrary; it was her uncle's fiftieth birthday celebration that took place on the opposite side of town. She knew that even if the party ended at one or two-o-clock in the morning her parents would stick around to help clean up and socialize with remaining guests that lingered. She knew her parent's routine like the back of her hand and timed it perfectly. Twinkles was ready for bed but she could not sleep. Her parents got home about a half hour after her. They checked on her and wondered why she was still awake; and then they went to bed without their usual night chatter that she frequently overheard since their bedroom was above hers but on the second level. This time her parents fell asleep by the time their heads hit their pillows.

By the way, the club owner would have gotten into serious trouble because it had a reputation of not only permitting minors under twenty-one entry access; but they also served liquor to minors. This contributed to why Twinkles felt a sense of entitlement: she was young, attractive, and charismatic and people were always relaxed in her presence. However, no nineteen-year-old should have been allowed entrance into a nightclub that served liquor to anyone under twenty-one because it's against the law (at least it is illegal in the United States).

Twinkles decided to go into the living room to watch TV with the volume turned down low since she was restless. Less than ten minutes later a loud bump, bump, bump was on the front porch. It startled her and what startled her more was the repetition of the ringing doorbell. She was almost afraid to check to see who made the raucous. She peeped through the peephole only to see Freckles wild with a bloody nose and panicked face. Freckles screams hysterically to her to open the door.

Needless to say, the twenty-seven-year-old man they'd met in the club had punched her in the face, pushed her out of her car and stole it with purse still inside. It was like a scene from a B-rated movie. Twinkles prayed her parents would sleep through this but no such luck. They called the police in the midst of the commotion who came and took a report. A different police officer actually found the guy and arrested him.

They got another patrol car to take Freckles home because she was too upset to drive even if they had recovered her car at that point. Thankfully, her car was later returned to her. One of the officers scoffed at Twinkles and accused her of not believing she'd done anything wrong. Her dad chimed in and discussed the dangers of picking up strangers, which angered Twinkles because she had to remind them that: #1 she wasn't the driver and couldn't control who the driver allowed inside her car; #2 she had warned Freckles about that guy and #3 she never had and never would pick up strangers! The police officer calmed down and expressed how his emphatic outburst came from a place of concern. He offered that she was beautiful and how it would have upset him if something bad had happened to her; and how it grieved him to do reports where others got hurt or worse as a result of picking up strangers.

Twinkles countered that she was not stupid. Neither was she a fool. She asked the officer if he noticed that Freckles was significantly older than her and he agreed that Freckles should have known better since she was indeed *older*. He said she may have been older, but she was not necessarily more mature or wiser. Twinkles did not comment but she thought to herself and knew the officer was right.

The news about Twinkles and Freckles spread like wildfire. Twinkles' phone rang off the hook the next day. Her best friend who was her peer had heard what happened through people that knew Freckles and was shocked to learn Twinkles was the "young friend" that had gone out with her the previous night. Twinkles felt horrible about what happened. She also felt guilty even though it was not her decision to chauffeur strange men they'd met in the club; especially considering she had forewarned Freckles about the bad neighborhood where the club was located. She pondered why such a fun night had to end tragically, though grateful it hadn't been any worse than it was.

She called to check on Freckles the next day but Freckles avoided seeing Twinkles after that tragic night. Freckles immediately transferred to a different department at work too. She lied and said it was a promotion but Twinkles knew it was a lateral move. Twinkles also knew Freckles was embarrassed about what happened but felt that wasn't reason enough to sever the friendship. Initially they had clicked and always had plenty to talk and laugh about; yet Twinkles, with hurt feelings and all, finally got a clue and moved on after Freckles constantly ignored her.

So young people, the purpose for this discussion is to remind you that you will always make mistakes so don't use your mistakes as a deterrent from reaching interpersonal goals. The point is to grow in wisdom and learn from other people's mistakes as well as your own. The aforementioned scenario demonstrates how the younger individual actually applied more wisdom in a situation that involved people that were chronologically older. Can you say the same? If you were in that position would you have chosen wisdom? Would you have chosen to use your leisure time more constructively? Do you really think it's wise to meet your "boo" in a nightclub? This may not apply to those that may not be looking for their soulmates. Neither is this to say it's never okay to meet someone at a club. This is to say you should take precaution wherever you meet someone particularly if it's a stranger from a club.

Personally, I wished I had a professional mentor when I was in my teens and twenties. I wished there was someone in my life that directed me to others in my age group that participated in more constructive hobbies and cultural activities such as classical music concerts, museums and how to develop into a more well-rounded individual. If I'm being truthful here I also wished there was someone in my young life that connected me with more people in my age group that understood the significance of a personal relationship with God. Or, I wished there were people in my life that understood the significance of a personal spiritual relationship with the Lord. My mom, grandma and great-great grandmother were church goers. No disrespect intended but there is so much more to spirituality than only going to church. I learned about God's expectation and religion from home life and school. However, the significance of developing a personal relationship with the Almighty is something I did not learn about until after I got married. I wished for a spiritual mentor because I believe if I had learned spiritually on a higher level in my teens I may have had a better sense of self as well as made wiser decisions that affected more than just myself. I don't regret how things turned out…it's just that sometimes I cannot help but wonder, "what if?"

What if Iyanla Vanzant was around during my teens and I had the opportunity to meet and be mentored by her. She's amazing – she reeks of wisdom. She's spiritual. She seems to be a straight shooter, she seems to be direct, which is something I respond to well. I like direct people because there's usually no room for ambiguity when dealing in directness.

I've interjected this discussion regarding Minister Vanzant because while her television show deals mostly with family/

marital issues, I believe young people could learn a lot about life by paying attention to her wisdom. Freckles' marriage may have been salvaged if she had Iyanla or someone like her in her life. Freckles and Twinkles might still be friends because she may have been home with her family as opposed to gallivanting out to nightclubs with Twinkles.

The point, young people, is simply to encourage you to think and apply wisdom in every area of your life – it could save you from making critical mistakes and help you avoid severe consequences.

Furthermore, you who may not believe in God per se must not be angered by perspectives influenced by spirituality. I'm sure most of us follow our own minds with or without ethereal inspiration. Although I will sporadically mention God or spirituality; I will also frequently remind you that I'm not here to proselytize or assume you believe in a higher power. I'm only sharing thoughts I believe to be positive, enriching and have the potential to add value to your life as they have truly added value to my life and others who have crossed my path.

I'm reminded of another incident of a know-it-all youth that happened a couple of years ago. I drove our nephew (who my husband I had custody of since he was twelve after his mother passed away) downstate to his college registration and move-in day. It was an exciting time in his life and I had already experienced this with our sons yet the feelings of observing young people move towards the next chapter of their lives never gets old to me.

We waited outside in line for instructions for what seemed to take an eternity. Finally, his name was called and we received a printout that advanced us to the next long line that led to the dorm assignment. The staff instructions were concise and called you according to your last name to follow the strategically placed arrows that helped get you to your next destination – I was actually impressed by how organized things were for such a massive campus.

I noticed a young lady who was with her parents. The dad was people watching but the mom was fuming and yelled at the young lady, who by the context of the conversation, was her daughter. The mother said, "That's your problem you don't like to listen. You think you know every \*\*##@@$%%\*\* thing but you don't know s\*\*\*! You think you're so \*\*\*###% grown. You betta not waste my money…since you think you're so grown you better show me how grown you are and make passing grades or else I'm going come up to this school and kick your ass if you flunk any classes." Needless to say, Mama was angry!

I tried to turn away as the young lady gave me quick eye contact that read embarrassment. It took everything within me not to laugh out loud because I understood the mother's position. It was hot that day and people were everywhere. We had just been instructed where to go next when the young lady, who acted like a spoiled know-it-all little girl, told her parents to go in the opposite direction. Her mother gently pled with her and pointed in the correct direction but the girl stubbornly refused to listen. I wondered why the girl challenged her mother who looked like the type not to be reckoned with; but before I could get my thought out the mother metaphorically pounced on the girl by using strong words.

I wanted to feel sorry for the girl but I didn't because she wasted time and caused them to lose their place in line. They would have been further along if she had listened to her mother, who at the beginning was patient and nice. It wasn't until the girl spoke disrespectfully that the mother went off on her. What made it laughable is the mother didn't care that she went off on her in public. The mother continued to make comments to the effect that she hopes the girl would be just as smart in her classes as she had been with her big mouth. As a parent and legal guardian, I totally relate to the mother. My sons and my nephew never liked to listen to the voice of reason, nor the voice of wisdom, while growing up. They knew everything; but my husband and I who've been in the world almost twice as long as them knew nothing. Not so!

All of our children are now young adults. I no longer try to influence decisions they make no matter how wrong those decisions are. I sometimes slip up and give unsolicited advice; but experience, for the most part, has taught me to let them make their own mistakes even though I frequently cringe in the inside about many of their decisions. I've learned over and over that the more nurturing and caring I am the more resistance they render. I desperately desire for them not to suffer through the agony of obvious mistakes; but usually they don't see it as me trying to help until it's too late. I now offer my shoulder and my ear and without the "I told you so" adage; in fact, they're usually the ones that say, "I should have listened to you Ma/ Aunty." It seems the older they get the more they appreciate my efforts, this might be because I've learned to back off; plus, they know how much I love them and that I'm always here for them. It may also be because they're growing in wisdom, which is great.

Earlier we learned Twinkles was not the blame for what happened to her friend, Freckles, but she made her fair share of mistakes in an unrelated incident that involved her boyfriend. Twinkles is now a few years older and only goes to clubs for special occasions like a friend's birthday or wedding reception. She partied so much in her late teens that by the time she was actually old enough to legally go to clubs she had lost interest.

As fate would have it she was invited to an upscale club to attend a friend's birthday party. She wasn't in the mood for the club scene but Twinkles was a loyal friend if nothing else so she went. She reconnected with a guy she met years before and truly believed fate had reconnected them. He was a pretty boy that drank too much.

They quickly fell in love and she enjoyed having him on her arm. She was invited to a prestigious fashion show and looked forward to showing off her new beau. They went on double dates with other friends and always had a good time. She introduced him to her grandmother because she knew she couldn't be objective about possible character flaws he may have possessed, in addition to drinking too much. Granny on the other hand, saw straight through him and outright told her to be careful because, "He was a slick one." Twinkles trusted her grandmother's judgment and asked if she felt he would ever hurt her. Her grandmother didn't believe he'd ever physically harm her – yet love and desire tipped the scales of the reality of her grandmother's "mama wit." Although Twinkles trusted her grandmother's "mama wit" which here refers female intuition and wisdom; she felt that as long as he would never physically hurt her she was in capable hands. Ironically, she simultaneously appreciated her grandmother's caveat about him being a little slick. She reasoned in her mind that she didn't have to worry about him ever trying to run game on her since he was the one who stated it was fate that reconnected them. Yep, she believed his hype.

To play it safe Twinkles also introduced him to her play aunt and uncle. She told her play aunt to be honest with her opinion about him because he could be the one! Thankfully her aunt and uncle immediately liked him and gave her their seal of approval.

There was an upcoming event that she only wanted to attend if her man could join her. He wanted to join her but said he didn't have anything to wear. Twinkles had **A** #1 credit and bought him a new suit from Baskins, which for those of you who are familiar know the suit was not cheap. Back then Baskins honored Chas. A. Stevens credit card, which was one of her favorite department stores for women. Twinkles wasn't apprehensive about buying the suit and told her boyfriend to pay her back whenever he could. She felt she was being a "modern woman" by shopping for her man. She especially wanted him to look good for the event where all her friends would be checking him out and discussing fashion; she bought a knockout dress for herself that complemented his suit. They made a fierce couple and she knew it!

One month had passed since the event and there was no mention of him reimbursing her for the cost of the suit. She knew she hadn't put a specific timeframe on it but thought the gentlemanly thing to do would be for him to confirm he had intended on paying her back. It didn't occur to her at this point that a red flag should have immediately gone up in her mind about his character. She dismissed it in her mind and felt that the suit would be his birthday present if they were still together by the time his birthday rolled around.

It was Friday night and Twinkles looked forward to seeing her man. He said he couldn't pick her up because they lived miles apart and his car was in the shop. She had a new 5-speed and offered to pick him up so they could hang out and he agreed without hesitation. He lived a solid hour and thirty minutes away and it took forever for her to get to his place, which was actually his parent's home. He'd explained how his ex-wife took him to the cleaners for child and spousal support which is why he had to move back with his parents until he got back on his feet. She believed he was divorced because she met his aging parents who were Christians. They liked her instantly mostly because they learned she was a church goer and enjoyed discussing the Bible though her knowledge of it was limited.

They went to the upscale club where they met, which she usually only tolerated but any amount of time she spent with her man was time well spent. They got takeout food after the club and came back to her place for a nightcap before it was time to drive him home. It was Friday night and after working all week long she was too tired to drive him all the way home and fell asleep watching TV. Even though the drive at this time of night would only take about 45 minutes instead of the usual hour in a half it took during rush hour traffic she was relieved when he asked if he could drive himself home and return her car the next day after he got off work. He stated that would help him since his car, a beautiful corvette, was in the repair shop. She *trusted* him and let him take her car.

The next day was Saturday and she decided to sleep in; she wouldn't have been able to go too far since he had her car. She called him around 5 P.M. to find out what time to be ready. He was supposed to call after his shift ended around three but this didn't bother her because she understood that his route sometimes took longer if he had to wait for a manager to become available to sign-off on his delivery sheet. He earned a decent salary as a truck driver for a well-known cola company.

Okay, it's now seven o'clock in the evening…nine o'clock… midnight and she still hadn't heard from him. She is suddenly panicked stricken because she thinks he's been in an accident and too banged up to call. She called his parents but didn't get an answer, which confirms her worries – she now believes he's laid up in some hospital too banged up to call; neither did his parents call because they didn't have her phone number. Why oh why didn't she just get up and drive him home?!! Twinkles is sick with worry to her core.

A few more days have passed and she didn't hear from him. She's beyond panic mixed with some anger that she tries to suppress at least until she learns if he's okay. She contemplates which one of her friends to ask to drive her to his parent's house because she would not know how to get there by train, or if there's a stop on his end that's close to his parents' house. It bugs her to have to tell anyone that he's M.I.A. let alone the fact that he has her car; but it's the middle of a new week now and she knows she cannot put it off any longer. She attempts to call him one more time before she asks one of her friends to drive her to Rockford from Chicago.

He unexpectedly picks up the phone on the tenth ring. She could hear distress and hesitation in his voice. Her heart palpitates as she listens to the news that he'd wrecked her car. She asks if he's okay because she assumed he was laid up in some hospital all banged up with bandages from head to toe. That was not the case. He was too much of a coward to call to explain what happened mostly because he'd been drinking when he totaled her car. He met his brother at a neighborhood bar after he left her apartment last Friday, the Friday she had been too tired to drive. The Friday before the Saturday he had to be at work early in the morning. Yeah right!

She affirmed that he shouldn't have been afraid to tell her what happened because that's what's insurance is for; she told him she'd take the car to a couple of mechanics to get repair estimates. He said he would reimburse her for the deductible which never happened! He dodged her until finally she went out to his house. She explained to his parents what had happened and they had not been aware that he wrecked her car let alone pay for damages; yet they agreed he was responsible for paying the insurance deductible.

She saw him sneak around back as she was leaving. He tried to avoid her but she doubled back to confront him. He lied in her face in the presence of his parents and said the only reason why she wanted him to pay for damages was because he'd broken things off with her. She countered and said it was the first of her hearing that they were no longer a couple and that was fine she said, "Just give me my money for the deductible!"

Twinkles never recovered her money for her car or for the suit. Ladies, learn from Twinkles mistake and never be overly generous to a man. Anytime a man eagerly accepts expensive gifts, money and/or asks for a loan; he could very well be a poor excuse for a man! A real man does not take from a woman.

Maybe it's okay to be super generous if you don't give more than you can stand to lose. This was not the case for Twinkles. Having to come up with the $500 deductible set her back. She earned enough to comfortably take care of herself as an administrative assistant; but she essentially lived from paycheck-to-paycheck and saved very little. She had rent, car payments and loved to dress well and there was little room to be splurging on anyone else.

The exception to the rule may be if you're wealthy. I don't know because even wealthy people seem to grow tired of always giving and never receiving. I've personally met women on both sides of the coin. I've met women who suffer from being overly generous to men as in the case of Twinkles. And, I've also witnessed women that don't mind financially supporting men; in fact, these women don't mind because many of them use money as a means of control but that's another story. My advice is simply to think things through before acting on them.

And guys, you likewise have to be watchful of opportunistic women. If she only comes around when it's your payday a red flag should go up in your mind. Does she enjoy spending time with you on the regular? Or is she always tired until it's your payday? These are thoughts worthy of consideration before you dole out your hard earned cash.

Young people please understand that you have the rest of your life to make grownup decisions. Why rush it? I frequently tell our college aged children, "You're going to be grown until you die so you will have a lifetime of making decisions on your own. It gets old...one day you'll be glad to let someone else share the decision-making responsibility...so be cool and enjoy your young life."

Another true scenario is of a youth I know that went away to college and became buck wild. I won't say the person's gender but let's refer to him/her as Dana since Dana can either be masculine or feminine. Here is "Dana's" story:

Dana has always been smart academically and had no problem entering a respectable college. Dana connected with new friends and majored in partyology 101 but somehow was able to maintain decent grades until he/she was offered a marijuana cigarette at a party, which took Dana to a different dimension. Dana started purchasing pot only to discover it did not have the same effect he/she previously experienced. Dana was not given marijuana but PCP and became a junkie and ended up in jail.

There are so many more details to Dana's life. Youngsters, do you really want to throw your life away and risk ending up in jail for a cheap thrill? PCP aged Dana over a short period of time that seemed to occur overnight. I would cry inside because I know how much potential Dana had if he/she had stayed on the narrow path.

Many college kids experiment; myself included. But as we see in Dana's story one little experiment changed the course of his/her life. Dana does not have that fabulous career and life but is struggling according to the last update I heard from a family member.

I mentioned I experimented the first time I went away to college and can honestly say I never enjoyed being intoxicated off anything especially marijuana. It simply did not feel normal to me and I thank God I didn't like it because who knows, maybe my life would have taken a different course if I enjoyed being under the influence. It's normal to be curious yet I strongly suggest to youth not to try or sample it! Trust me, being high is not all that. I venture to say that anytime your "friends" are trying to persuade you into experimenting it's because they see your potential and want to drag you down. They have nothing constructive to offer and don't want to see you get ahead. Or, they are simply too insecure to go it alone and want you to be silly with them. It's just not worth it. People glamorize being high as something cool, but the reality is that substances age you as you saw in chapter 5 so why chance aging prematurely? I repeat, it's not worth it! Please trust me on this.

I believe youth misunderstand older adults and think we want to be in your business and constantly tell you what to do but you're wrong! Most adults understand that it is our job to manage and guide you not rule over you. We know you are individuals with your own ideas and interests. I believe it's also safe to assume that most of us know the importance of allowing you to spread your wings. Furthermore, we also know that no amount of micro-managing will prohibit you from making your own mistakes. What we know with certainty is that if you do a better job of listening to us instead of rebelling you will be better prepared for life…the real world where you will be required to regularly make decisions.

As for me, I frequently shared with my children about how my mistakes detained me in life in hopes that by expressing my previous mistakes could encourage them to make better choices in their lives. Regret is a useless emotion but it doesn't mean I don't think about how my life would have turned out if I had done a better job of listening to wisdom. Although I didn't have a business mentor there were people in my life that gave good advice, including my parents. People closest to you don't always know how to effectively communicate, which is how many of us miss what might be great counsel. Either way, if we are as clever as we think we are we must find a way to absorb wisdom from whatever hand we are dealt in life. Instead of exuding rebellion if you don't like what's being said, be silent and think about how what's being said can actually benefit you.

Don't be like the young lady who didn't pay attention to the wisdom (or common sense in this case) of her mother until her mother snapped off on her. Neither be like the Freckles, the thirty-four-year-old that was incapable of seeing a hoodlum for who he truly was. Perhaps if she had turned off her nurturing nature for two seconds that could have been long enough for her to realize she was dealing with a thug and poor excuse for a man. Consequently, don't be overly generous like Twinkles was to a boyfriend who took no accountability for wrecking her car nor did he reimburse her for the suit she purchased.

Do you really want to be that person who only listens when someone curses at you? Or will a police officer have to escort you home because you had no discernment about the impending danger from a thug? I should hope not. Sometimes silence truly is golden so be quiet, slow to speak, but quick to accept the wisdom offered from those that truly care about you.

It's my understanding that children who have been adopted or have foster parents have experiences that others don't. Some may even experience rejection; but I'm here to encourage you not to feel rejected. Don't feel that your life would have definitely been better if your birth parents had raised you. That would be like saying birth parents never abuse their own children and we know this simply is not true. Many birth parents have been arrested for child abuse. Please appreciate it if you are fortunate and have loving adopted or foster parents. They love you deeply and love is love no matter if it's from birth, adopted, or foster parents. There are foster kids in the system that get tossed from home to home and desire stability. I bet they'd do practically anything to have a stable life in any form. Therefore, if you are one of the fortunate ones, please appreciate what you have.

On the other hand, if you don't have stability, make it your life's mission to do well in school, stay out of trouble and respect academic counselors and other authorities in a position to help you.

There's an older song entitled *I'll Be Loving You Always* by Stevie Wonder on his 1976 hit album *Songs in the Keys of Life*. A portion of the lyrics within this particular song goes: *We all know sometimes life's hates and troubles, can make you wished you were born in another time and space, but you can bet your life times that and twice its double, God knew exactly where he'd wanted you to be placed...* I dedicate this portion of the song to all that feel as though they were a mistake. You are not and were not a mistake! If you are in the midst of a hard childhood, please hold on; you will not be a minor forever. Take your negative and turn it into a positive. Journal daily. Later in life you could start a movement for the betterment of foster and adopted children. Later in life if you recognize adversity in the life of another child you can directly relate to what they're going through and offer him/her your support.

Young people please seriously take what you've just read into consideration and develop a desire, a pattern and a heart for listening and learning. Know that the learning process continues in adulthood. The late Maya Angelou was frequently quoted saying that she's always learning and would continue to learn until the day she dies. She lived to be 86! (If memory serves me correctly she was past sixty when she voiced the significance of always being a learner.) And, if a senior citizen can consider herself a learner, young people, including teens and youth in their twenties, can most certainly have a learner's attitude as opposed to a know-it-all attitude.

Youth and adults alike must be careful to listen to that still inner voice. Unwise choices have the potential to emotionally drain you and serve as one more deterrent that keeps one from goals or slows down the goal-achieving process. The true inner voice never disappoints because all who listen and follow it are more often than not glad they did. They may also avoid some headaches.

As prefaced earlier in this chapter, I love young people and interact with them frequently. My purpose here is to let you know in love that it's okay to listen, learn and be respectful to adults that have authority over you. Respect is likewise a two-way street that is, it should be from youth to elders and from elders to youth. We must listen to one another and learn from one another and know that much can be accomplished when we interact with each other respectfully.

# Nine

## Murphy's Law in Effect, Obstacles Exist: How Bad Do You Want It?

*N*o one escapes the curveballs that life sometimes throws. This assumes you live on planet Earth. Wouldn't it be lovely if we had everything we wanted at our disposal? I'm not sure that's what's best but one can certainly dream! The reality is that stuff happens. The other reality is sometimes it seems no matter what we do we cannot overcome what seems to be untimely obstacles. You've almost made it to the next plateau and then bam, life unexpectedly gets in the way and it seems you're going two steps backwards instead of a tiny step forward. The question is this: how bad do you want peace of mind? You thought the question would ask how bad you want success, wealth, or something of the like. It's okay to desire success and even wealth; in spite of this you also need to understand that no amount of success, wealth, and the like can be enjoyed if you don't first possess peace of mind. Murphy's Law mandates that peace of mind is impossible because whenever things start to improve something stops it from coming full circle; but we're going to consider that peace of mind is absolutely attainable! With or without obstacles!!

I hesitate to discuss the meaning of Murphy's Law because its nature is negative and I'm all about being positive and having a positive outlook in life. It's challenging for those of us that grew up in a negative environment to have a positive outlook mostly because the negativity became habitual and even though deep down inside you want to tear away from it you may be surrounded by people who are too negative to help. Then enters Murphy's Law which is the principle that says if it is possible for something to go wrong, it will go wrong. Here's what I say to Murphy's Law: I rebuke you in the name of Jesus! You can chant this as a positive affirmation even if you're not Christian!!

It never ceases to amaze me that people in general seem to embrace negativity faster than positivity. Some prefer to see the glass as half-empty and cannot change unless they undergo an exorcism or some other life altering phenomenon.

I've seen situations where friends had fun parties with a huge turnout only to complain about the no shows. Forget about those that actually showed up and enjoyed themselves; it's more comfortable to highlight those that didn't or couldn't make it. This may seem sarcastic but it's true for those who don't know how to appreciate what's already within their grasps. Sometimes we are so comfortable with negativity that we allow it to overshadow the positive, which is unfortunate.

Personally, I make it my mission in life to be content. Sure, I've been known to complain when I'm overwhelmed but it's taken me years to deeply understand that no amount of complaining, though complaining can oftentimes be liberating, has ever solved any of my problems. I lied to myself saying that complaining is good because it's therapeutic – maybe for some it is soothing; but complaining is not the answer. Sooner or later the people we complain to grow tired of hearing it and justifiably so. And, this doesn't discount the fact there are times we need to vent; but if we vent too much it turns into complaining, which is unacceptable!

I've had a couple of close friends in my life that welcomed me to vent about problems. Don't fall for this! Meditate and pray over your problems or pay a professional therapist to listen and help you sort through problems because most people that are not professional therapists or social workers don't qualify to advise you. And, more often than not they will grow tired of listening to your problems especially if you're complaining about the same things over and over.

My two friends were eager to listen to my problems, which at the time was about my husband who was working my nerves big time! These friends didn't know each other. Friend #1 was present during the early stages of my marriage. She had already been married a few years and I figured she had more experience, as well as seemed to have a solid marriage and I thought I could benefit from her seemingly expertise. She encouraged me to share my problems and gave good counsel but guess what? One day at the beginning of our conversation she boldly stated, "If you're going to talk about something bad I don't want to hear it." You could have knocked me over with a feather! My friend who'd always been available to listen to me vent turned on me at the drop of a dime. Even now some fifteen plus years later I still feel in retrospect she could have been gentler in her delivery about not desiring to hear me vent. I would have understood that she grew tired of hearing me complain but she hurt my feelings to my core mostly because from the beginning it was her who encouraged me to share my problems. Rest assuredly I never complained to her again for the duration of our friendship.

I had vented to her on a large scale because I did not know how to overcome the issues I was dealing with at that time. She was devoted to the friendship but inwardly grew tired of hearing me complain, which I was clueless about until she insulted me in a most insensitive manner. I almost cried but my inner stubbornness wouldn't allow for tears. Instead I decided not to share anything with her except praiseworthy news. I felt like such a phony but it's what I did and she noticed the shift in me and frequently asked about Tim and my retort was always positive even if Tim and I had just got done arguing.

Friend #2, another close friend, let me vent and complain. This time the problems were different but still brought me to a point of anger. The problem discussed with Friend #2 was nowhere as serious as the problem discussed with Friend #1. The problem with Friend #1 had to do with how vulnerable I felt after a miscarriage. At the time, I felt my husband had left me alone too much considering my physical and mental state. I was upset that it took what seemed an eternity to conceive only for it to end up in miscarriage.

I interject that I was too trusting of both friends. They weren't gossips but neither did they exactly keep every conversation totally confidential. The good news is that neither friend knew the friends I grew up with so even if they slipped up it would not have gotten back to my childhood friends. The better news is that I harbor no resentments and they will always be my friends. My friendships with Friends #1 and #2 never crossed paths – they had never met each other.

Reluctantly I shared with Friend #2 because she was not a gossip…or so I thought. I frequently asked her if she was tired of me complaining and she always replied that it didn't bother

her. I didn't want to repeat overly complaining as I had done with Friend #1. Friend #2 had never been married and this should have been reason enough for me not to overly expose my marital woes. The one thing about her is that I don't believe she kept the deepest things I shared with her about my marriage and other secrets in total confidence. If I've misjudged her integrity than shame on me because I know for a fact that she did not actually keep every detail between us.

I confided to her that about three years into our marriage my husband had asked me to sign some separation or divorce papers; I honestly don't recall the exact legality of the papers. I recall that it specifically said that by signing on the dotted line I agree to walk away from the marriage with nothing. He and I had been arguing and it truly didn't make since to stay together especially since this was before our children were born (not that I believe children should be the sole reason why couples should stay together). I shared with Friend #2 how angry I was because I felt that my husband had insulted my intelligence by asking me to sign something in the heat of an argument without first consulting an attorney.

I told my husband to let me hire an attorney to look at the papers before signing and he insisted that I didn't need to do that; but the sooner I'd sign the sooner he would be out of my life. There was plenty more arguing and finally I signed. I said, "Give me the damn papers!" I didn't sign my name; instead I signed "F--- You"! He thought he had the victory until he realized it wasn't my signature on the papers. Friend #2 cracked up with laughter when I told her that was how I handled it. (For the record, the account of my marriage was from the rough patches during the early stages of marriage – my husband Tim was and still is a great provider for his family.)

Fast forward to years later she got married and suffered marital woes. She later told me in a conversation that she shared with her colleagues the actual obscenity I'd signed instead of my signature. She stated that she hadn't given away any details about my situation but how befitting it was to their conversation. A mental flag was instantly raised in my mind but for whatever reason I never challenged her about what she revealed to her work buddies, some of whom I'd actually met. It could have most likely been because in the midst of sharing about her own problems she may have inadvertently mentioned my obnoxious behavior for instant comic relief.

The marriage of Friend #2 failed. It didn't last six months. It had been easy for her to render marital advice to me who had already been married at least three years at the time when she didn't apply her own advice past one year. I knew her marriage wouldn't last because her husband was more obnoxious than mine (forgiven the temporary negativity). He was selfish and unyielding and I told my friend that I hoped he would not end up braking her heart because there was something ruthless and untrustworthy about him that I immediately sensed. Everyone, that is, everyone except me, thought they'd make it because they had a lot in common and were *seemingly* compatible. Not to be negative but I knew from the depths of my being it wouldn't work and my intuition never lies to me. I desperately wanted my friend to be happy because she is a very reasonable person who is not impulsive and usually thinks things through. She didn't have that desperation women frequently possess when there doesn't seem to be any viable marriage prospect in their immediate future. She crossed all the t's and dotted all the i's on her checklist of husband prospects; yet her marriage failed miserably.

Her husband and I did not get along. He was conversational and friendly toward me when we initially met; yet for whatever reason he got annoyed with me because he felt I talk too much. He asked me at some point if I ever got tired of talking. I retorted, "Unlike quiet sneaky people I talk a lot because I don't have anything to hide." Boom! That'll teach him not to ever insult me.

I didn't hold back but was honest and expressed my feelings about him to my friend; yet she married him anyway…

I was there for Friend #2 and continue to be available for her to this day if she needs me. She was determined that no man, husband or otherwise, would bring her down. I actually admire her for her strength and continued to confide minor annoyances in my marriage, which probably wasn't smart; even though the stuff I'd complain about was petty and nonthreatening. It got to the point that whenever I attempted to share with her she'd interrupt me midsentence to tell me that I was wrong for this or that. My response would frequently be I know I'm wrong and I said wrongful and harsh things in anger. I asked her not to judge me but just simply let me be expressive.

Friend #2 was incapable of letting me vent without judging me. What's interesting is that it angered her whenever a mutual friend of ours judged her actions in her marriage; yet she always felt compelled to judge me then deny the fact that she was being judgmental. She never owned that she was overbearing, insensitive and judgmental. She said that she has a very analytical mind and asks a lot of questions in order to analyze situations. I countered and said you can dress it up any way you want it; it's still the equivalence of being overbearing, unsympathetic, as well as judgmental instead of being a good friend towards me during my time and need of emotional support. This may sound harsh on my part and perhaps it was a little harsh; I felt and still feel that I allow friends to be themselves because no one is perfect. I accept people for who they are and if they say or do something I don't agree with I politely let them know how I feel. I simply wanted her to own it. She was unreasonable but denied it and that was what did not settle well with me. Even if she had admitted that she could sometimes be the person I described I would have accepted that she was owning up to being judgmental among other things. She was also nosy but that didn't bother me as much mostly because I believe everyone has a degree of curiosity or they are outright nosy...I'm talking about Gladys Kravitz nosy (the neighbor from *Bewitched* the television sitcom). Anyone that denies this is either a liar or is in straight up denial.

We should all practice courtesy in relationships if for no other reason than the fact that we all go through situations where we need to vent. For those of us that keep things inside as opposed to venting, you might want to be careful about that. You may think it's safe to keep stuff inside because you don't want to risk being judged or ridiculed by others. Some of us may not vent because we don't trust family members or friends enough to share for fear the ones you share with may go back and gossip in the same manner in which you've gossiped about others. My recommendation is that if this describes you, stop gossiping so that you're free to share info without distrusting others. Unlike I did in the aforementioned actions of my experience with friends 1# and 2#, exercise wisdom in what you share or at least share with a professional. Either way, we must feel free to vent and not keep things that bother us bottled up inside.

Murphy's Law can be multifaceted if not nipped in the bud. It can happen in friendships, marriage, workplace and life in general; but we must properly deal with this negative mindset before it becomes a perpetual state of life. We accomplish this by the manner in which we handle situations. We mustn't allow anyone to rain on our parade. It's pathetic that in some circles people seem to enjoy seeing others in hard dilemmas and struggling. Even some friendships are established because the befriender welcomes the opportunity to live and enjoy the negativity of the one whose friendship they pursue. Then heaven forbids the one whose friendship they pursue gets on their feet and start doing well in life. The pursuer inwardly feels betrayed because they used to feel superior to the one they considered to be a lowly person that was once bombarded with life's struggles. Now the one previously perceived as lowly has become victorious and overcame obstacles that the one who previously felt superior didn't perceive could ever be accomplished. The pursuer should be happy for the person who conquered obstacles but is subconsciously (or perhaps consciously) resentful of the victor's victory.

I took this detour down the valley of the Mississippi, that is, I went off course in order to encourage you at your current age to block negativity or thoughts of Murphy's Law. Murphy's Law mandates defeat and you are not defeated! Don't feel trapped if you're underage and still live with parents that may not understand how to be positive. Be inwardly determined to be a positive person no matter what your environment is. How, you may ask? The way to become a positive person is by negating every negative thought, thing, or action delivered by others as well as the negative thoughts you may conjure in your own mind. Adverse situations and negative internal thoughts might arise, but do not entertain negativity. Replace that negative thought with a happy thought or experience – this is how you redirect your mindset. You can do it! I have faith in you.

I've met people of all ages that have overcome unbelievable obstacles because they were determined to focus their attention on the positive. You must tell yourself that if others can do it; so can you! Minors, this isn't an invitation to be rude to your parents. You must be respectful and understand that one day you will be a full-grown adult and have many opportunities to make independent decisions, but until then, redirect your mindset towards positivity.

For adults over twenty-one: you're too old to possess a mindset that prohibits you from utilizing your full potential of the growth as well as development of a decent character. You are not the first person to have problems. Everyone experiences setbacks. What separates you from overcoming setbacks is your negative mindset and lack of determination. Poor me, everyone picks on me all the time. If this is you stop it! You've whined long enough so pick yourself up by first determining within yourself to possess a positive mindset, create a plan even if you need to solicit help from someone, then finally, see your plan through with relentless determination until it succeeds! All the help in the world will not help you if you are not determined to change that negative Murphy's Law way of thinking. Besides, haven't you grown tired of living in a constant state of misery? If you're tired of being miserable start by changing how you think; otherwise you may actually be comfortable living in a continuous state of misery and if this is true you don't have anyone to blame but yourself. Stop thinking negatively. Stop dwelling in your pity parties. And if you can't move past it don't bring other people down, stay in your pity party by yourself!!

There are times even now that life overwhelms me. My father died the day after Christmas and was memorialized January 3, 2015. He was in hospice the last several months of his life and in and out of the emergency room before hospice. He lived with my younger brother until he was admitted into hospice. There was plenty of family drama, which also happened around the time I experienced not getting my dream job and my youngest son had been rushed to the emergency room to a hospital near the town in Ohio where he went to college. These are just a few highlights of all that I was suffering simultaneously. Not too much is more alarming than to receive a call at 2:30 A.M. from the university's dean who delivered the bad news. My husband and I got up in the middle of the night and drove to Ohio to make sure our son was okay. Thankfully my son is now okay and taking a break from the stress of college life. If there was ever a time I wanted to have a pity party, it was then.

I've learned to relax regarding my dream job. My husband does an excellent job of holding down the financial fort. I could have continued to bellyache about not having my own money with the mindset that mandates "there's nothing like having your own money"; or I could create my own opportunity. I chose the latter.

Most of what I do is volunteer, which I enjoy but don't generate an income. I enjoy ministry work but one mustn't enter ministry work for the money. Maybe Joel Osteen, Creflo Dollar, Joyce Meyer, Tony Evans and TD Jakes are exceptions but it might be safe to assume that most ministry workers earn a modest income, if any income at all. Personally, I don't believe any of the just mentioned are in it just for the money. I believe they most likely never imagined that their ministries would be as successful as they are; but if I were a betting woman I'd bet the mindsets of these successful ministries started with positivity, much prayer and an above average work ethic. I'd bet there was no room for a Murphy's Law mindset for these ministry moguls. Neither should there be room for the Murphy Law effect in our mindset.

Since my income is modest I could have a pity party all day long or accept a job solely for the income as opposed to fulfillment. Instead I choose to trust the universe to turn my situation around and believe that I will someday earn my desired income. Besides, I've had jobs that paid well but I was miserable. My prayer is that no one ever has to be forced to accept a job solely because it pays well; my confidence and positive outlook says we won't only have to work to generate income – we will generate an income by doing something that we enjoy and something that helps others! Further, I believe the ministers that pastor mega-ministries become financially successful because they did not think about wealth when they initially began their ministries. Perhaps for them the wealth that came later was the unexpected icing on the cake, which added to a purpose that's been fulfilled through their ministries. I don't know this with certainty – this is just my theory based on how many lives they seem to positively touch.

I've learned to find the silver lining in situations until I get my desired results. I now appreciate the sun and the rain because both come with advantages. While the sun is aesthetically beautiful to view; the rain satiates the thirst that plant life requires which ultimately yields delicious fruits and vegetables for our consumption, not to mention beautiful flowers and greenery. If I'm always moaning about the rain I could never taste the wonderful fruit it produces.

Life gets hard for all at some time or another. The optimistic manner in which we respond is what gets us over the hump. It's what determines if we are going to develop as a result of challenges or if we going to accept obstacles as inevitable setbacks that keep us stuck, or worse, perish before any good thing happens. I prefer the former.

# Chapter

## *Ten*

## Trust Yourself

*H*ave you ever attempted to do something one way but decide to change your mind at the suggestion of another? Later you discover your original thought would have been more beneficial and now you're angry with yourself for not sticking to your original plan. If this describes you learn to listen to your gut instincts and trust them! Don't be capricious or double-minded because these suggest indecisiveness, lack of self-confidence and lack of focus.

I had a friend who confessed that if she had a quarter for every time she did this she'd be debt-free. There are plenty of opinionated people who think they know it all when in fact they may be experienced and knowledgeable but they don't know every detail about you and your situation. They should be listening instead of advising.

You fail yourself when you know in your heart that you should not marry that person even though he/she looks good on paper, or have a "banging body". Perhaps they are established in their careers, have good credit and are easy on the eyes, which are indeed adequate criteria. Maybe they're charismatic and others easily gravitate towards them due to their charm. This still isn't reason enough to marry them. Maybe they're different when you're alone. Initially they were charming to you but as you got to know them something shifted. Maybe they become easily annoyed and aloof when you're alone with them. Maybe they become sarcastic and unfriendly. It doesn't really matter. What matters is they are not the same around others as they are when it's just you. You initially ignored this because after all, they look good on paper. You convinced yourself that no one is perfect and maybe they're stressing about something that has nothing to do with you and you're simply being overly sensitive and unrealistic to expect them to behave the same way, to be "turned up" all the time. Your intuition warns you; in fact, it screams to you, "Run!" Instead you follow logic only to discover you've made an enormous mistake. You're one year into this friendship or relationship and are now convinced that you should have left them where you met them. Or worse you married them.

Another friend of mine, Friend #3, hated her professional job as an account manager. She worked with a group of lazy people who got away with murder because they'd been employees for years and were seldom challenged by the department head. They did just enough work to stay afloat; but they never went beyond the call of duty to assist the team members accomplish common goals for the entire department. Friend #3 always got stuck with intricacies that never allowed her to leave at quitting time. She worked long hours and no one cared. The one time she expressed how she felt she received a lack luster employee evaluation. This discouraged her from ever communicating how she felt again and future evaluations returned to being above average. The problem existed. She was burned out and kept headaches – stress related headaches.

One of her colleagues quit and went to work for a trendier company. Her colleague recommended her for a job that paid thirty percent more, which she gratefully accepted. Work related stress returned six months into her new job. She became physically ill because her new boss was cruel and misogynistic, her words not mine.

My confession is I was a little jealous of her new job because of the salary she earned and because she had long since completed her BA. I neither had a BA or MA at that time. Friend #3 was single with no children yet she earned more than my husband who had a family of four to support. I wasn't hostilely envious; yet it seemed as though everyone I knew had great careers and all I had was the routine life of raising children. I had no engaging conversation about high powered meetings, computer spreadsheets that needed amending, or award-winning stories I'd written to discuss. I hung out with fabulous people that seemed to enjoy my company but I always felt as though I never had anything interesting to contribute to conversations except the police stories my police officer husband had experienced and shared with me. Even those were his stories not mine. As I reminiscence, I'm sure many of the professional women I met through Friend #3 probably envied my life to a degree, if no more than the fact that as a stay at home mom I never had to deal with office politics, neither did I have work related stress. A couple of them were married but none of them had children. They'd frequently asked about my boys and the ones that met them commented on how well behaved they were, which is something that parents love to hear.

Friend #3 shared with me how ill she became. This concerned me and I demanded that she schedule an appointment to see a doctor, which she did and the doctor confirmed that her ailments were stress related and insisted that she at least take one week off from work. She reluctantly agreed but as soon as she returned to work the problems tripled. She cried on my shoulders daily. I felt like an idiot for the previous envy I felt because no amount of money is worth one's health.

Finally, I suggested that she consult a labor attorney. Her boss truly was misogynistic and mistreated his wife who was skinny and nervous. His wife would look in his direction before speaking and seemed scared to express humor whenever he invited his staff and friends to his home to celebrate the success of a fiscal year. They had a beautiful home but the atmosphere was cold. Friend #3 took my advice and her boss changed overnight after the labor attorney contacted the company's Human Resource department. My friend was awarded reimbursement for her medical bills, prescriptions for meds and a check for pain and suffering due to the stress her boss caused her to suffer; and the awarded fees also covered her attorney's expenses. They never even went to court! This well-known company did not want to risk its stellar reputation due to the actions of one insensitive boss. My friend thanked me profusely and took me to an expensive restaurant to show her gratitude. She solicited my help a few years later when she moved. All I did was carry a small lamp from her old residence to the new. She offered me money and I told her I didn't deserve to get paid because I hadn't done any heavy lifting. She insisted on paying me so I bought a picture from a street urchin that to this day hangs in my living room. It's a print but it's colorful and beautiful and I still love it. I couldn't wait to show it to her mostly because she thought I would spend it on my boys, whom I usually spent extras on, but this time I bought something that makes me smile every time I view it.

She eventually quit that stress induced position. The next job was stressful in that it had problems reaching its payroll – frequently the newer employees weren't paid on time. This was unheard of to me; to work and possibly not get paid on time. One thing I remember her saying is that at least at her old job she was paid for her stress and again she was forced to find another job. We lost contact over the years but it's my understanding from mutual friends that she is now gainfully employed with an established company. We're no longer in touch but I'm happy for her. And no, we did not have a falling out. Sometimes old friendships fade and new ones develop; it's just the way it is. I can't think of anyone from my past whose friendship would be unwelcomed by me today. Maybe if I thought about it extremely hard I could come up with at least one person who I would prefer to love from afar. I value friendship and would welcome a conversation from them as well; unless of course my gut tells me otherwise. It also goes without saying that I'd throw caution to the wind if I ever reconnected with a known gossip. Knowing me I'd befriend a gossiper but would know better than to share personal info with them; instead I'd minister to them and lead them towards being positive and constructive in how they communicate.

Friend #3 later confessed that she knew in her heart of hearts that she left her first job prematurely. She knew the reputation of that horrible boss but she had accepted that job because it paid more money. She had been anxious to leave because her coworkers took advantage of her work ethic. She literally did the job of three people and no one cared enough to help. In her mind she felt that she would show them by quitting when the next career opportunity came alone that in this case paid more money, was prestigious and one of the country's most desirable places to work. Unfortunately, what seemed to be an awesome opportunity ended up being a disaster. She went from the frying pan to the fire! Had she followed that still quiet voice inside it would have saved her from all she suffered. Sometimes I guess we must suffer a little agony before we reach our ultimate goals.

As stated earlier, my instincts never disappoint me. It is when I don't follow them that I suffer the consequences of disappointment.

There will be times when the grass will appear greener on the other side. Don't believe the hype. When you actually get to the other side you won't know the difference…at least not immediately. At least if you trust yourself with decisions and choices you may be able to experience inner victory with great results. If you listen to others against your better judgment and the results turn out unfavorable you will for sure kick yourself.

I've not met one person that hasn't said or inwardly felt "Something told me not to do that but I did it anyway and now I'm suffering." That "something" is your instincts…your inner voice. And yes, you most certainly should follow the instincts of that tiny sometimes loud voice, that tries to deter you away from mistakes even if you don't always immediately see the benefits of trusting your intuition. Sooner or later it will become clear as to why you should have trusted your instincts and you'll be thankful.

Someone dear and close to me confided to me and others in our circle that they married the wrong person. Their motives from the start were desperate. They weren't patient enough to wait on the right spouse and suffered in the worst way.

There are those that think things through and make great decisions. Wonderful! If this describes you, please be patient with others that don't possess your perspicacious characteristic. Many view situations the way we want them to be as opposed to how they actually are. There may not be an abundance of wisdom in this particular mindset yet people like this may require the wisdom and patience of others instead of possible condemnation or judgment. Using judgment is not the same as being judgmental so let this serve as a caveat against being critical to others. Besides, those of you that are loaded with wisdom haven't always possessed the wisdom that you now have. It's okay to allow others to make mistakes; it's how we all grow. It's unacceptable to influence others solely based on your outlook while totally ignoring the other person's state of mind. Maybe they are still developing in wisdom and are in the process of learning how to trust their instincts.

This is why we must learn to trust our own innermost thoughts. We must also not make decisions unilaterally based on emotions. Emotions are not the same as instincts. Emotions change like the weather; instincts are stable. Stability brings us closer to peace of mind, which is what most of us desire and/ or need. Following our emotions can lead to trouble. If the outcome of your decision ended negatively then it wasn't your instincts that you followed. It was most likely something else; perhaps it was an emotionally based choice of yours. Or perhaps it was the choice of another individual who negatively interfered and you chose to follow their unwise counsel, but their advice was not advantageous for you and it definitely was not your instincts if it ended up causing more damage than good.

We should learn from Esther's example of integrity and sound mind. She had to overcome many challenges; yet she remained focused and most importantly, trusted her *instincts*. Those familiar with the Old Testament's account of Esther's story in the biblical book of Esther recall how she was orphaned and raised by her elder cousin, Mordecai. The short version is Esther and her kin's people were Jewish and an evil government official named Haman hated all Jews and plotted to have them all exterminated. Esther and Mordecai found out about Haman's evil plans and had to take precautionary measures in communicating this info to King Xerxes because if one went before the king in those days with bogus information he or she could be executed on the spot if accusations against the king's right-hand man are determined to be false. In other words, truth had to be backed up with proof. Not to mention the fact that Esther is a woman and women had little autonomy during that era and she could have been as easily replaced as Vashti (you have to read or be familiar with the Book of Esther to understand this reference regarding Vashti).

Esther is nervous about her decision to inform the king about Haman's shenanigans BUT she is not governed by her nerves. Her *instincts* mandate the well-known verse, "...When this is done, I will go to the king even though it's against the law. And **if I perish I perish**." (KJV, Esther 4:16)

Esther was brave! We must likewise be brave and determined to follow our instincts. Moreover, we must trust that our instincts work to our advantage and others should think twice before attempting to counter our inner most wisdom. Learners of psychology refer to inner most wisdom as the Super Id, spiritual people may consider it as one's God-mind; it doesn't matter what you call it. Neither does it matter whether or not you're religious. What matters is that you should trust that a still inner voice exists within us and if we choose to follow it we will be better people for it.

Lastly, if I've said it once throughout this writing I've said it a hundred times: I am not trying to convert you! My desire is to share with you about the experiences of others (current day and historical characters of old) in hopes that you will benefit from these experiences or share with your loved ones who may benefit from the truths in this discussion.

# Chapter

# *Eleven*

## Reward Yourself

*We* unmistakably live in an era of quickness of motion. Our surroundings seem to be in a constant state of motion, especially if you live in the city. Cars, trains, buses, airplanes, helicopters, passersby, etc. We move quickly to keep up with life. We want things and we want them now...instant gratification, no time no patience. Life is short yet we bring new meaning to this cliché and seem to live each second in desperation. Granted, tomorrow isn't guaranteed but dang! Must we always be in such a hurry? Maybe yes for some of us.

We witness obnoxious drivers speeding through red lights and they most likely don't have to be anywhere that mandates putting other lives at stake all because they want to quickly get to their designations. We record favorite TV shows and zoom through commercials because we didn't want the plotline interrupted for a disruptive commercial in the first place.

How many of us, for example, warm our food in a conventional oven? Perhaps not too many; it's safe to assume most of us use microwave ovens. Most employers provide them in the office breakroom as well. Why? Because it's fast!

On a more serious note, those of us with kids rush from the time we get out of bed until the time we turn in for the night only to repeat the routine the next day assuming of course we make it to Friday before passing out. We wake the kids, get breakfast, make sure they have lunch money or lunchboxes, and drive them to school and then ourselves to work. The reality is we may already be tired by the time we get to work. Many school aged kids have afterschool activities that have to be factored into the daily routine. It's no wonder most of us plop on the sofa after a long and exhausting day. Oh wait, can't plop, what about dinner? McDonald's again today? Sounds like a good plan; we can finally sit down and put our feet up.

It's inevitable; we must roll with life. I suspect those that can afford to pay for housekeepers and nannies don't use their extra time to relax – they probably work longer hours or stay up late at night to complete the work brought home from the office. All the same, middle class, working class, upper middle class, or the wealthy; most everyone is super busy. Some are obnoxiously busy. Either way, we must move at the speed of light whether we want to or not.

Take time to be good to you! We all know for sure how taxing life can be and even if you are aware of this you must take time out for yourself. I'm sure I don't have to tell you what to do to relax. You know you've wanted to schedule that mani-pedi appointment but your busyness took you into overtime, you procrastinated and now you no longer have the time…or at least that's what you tell yourself. Maybe you should make time!

What about a Swedish massage? The right masseuse can make you feel as though you died and went to heaven. It doesn't matter if you can afford to make getting a massage a regular habit; treat yourself to one occasionally and you'll be glad you did. Look for a reputable online coupon for a half off deal if you have to because you deserve it.

Students, this applies to you also, whatever age you may be. Stress from writing research papers, studying subject after subject while trying to retain it all can be challenging for both high school and college students. Wondering which high school will accept the elementary aged student may also come with some stress. I returned to school later in life and had to learn to temporarily walk away from studying or writing when I became too overwhelmed especially when I pursued my masters of art degree.

I recall when I was about halfway through the master's program my oldest son, who was also in college, called home to see how I was doing. I express to him that I was miserable and tired of working on a paper that was eighty pages long not including footnotes and cover page. The writing wasn't the hardest part. Sifting through various reference books was what made the project more tedious. My back ached from sitting in the same positions for hours. I'd frequently typed from an upright position in my comfortable bed believing that would somehow make it more bearable; but that got old too or I became too comfortable and frequently fell asleep when I was supposed to be typing.

My son told me, "Ma, just get up and walk away from it for a couple of hours. Take a walk, get some exercise and when you return to it you'll have your second wind and will finish it." I told him I wanted to keep working because I didn't want to pull an all-nighter. He countered by saying what difference would that make if I was already miserable; this made sense. I took his suggestion and felt refreshed by the time I returned to complete the paper. Who knew someone I birthed had great wisdom? Lol. My grade for the paper was an A and I couldn't wait to inform him how his suggestion proved worthy.

It would have been easy for me to make excuses to quit. I could have told myself that I was too old for this school crap and gave up. Trust me there were many times I wanted to drop out because I felt I was too old to finish such an intense program. By this time, I had already earned a BA and that was good enough for me. Nevertheless, what is the theme of this publication? I advise readers to never use age as a deterrent from obtaining one's goals – right? I had to practice what I preach and I applied this advice to my own life – never use age as a deterrent from setting and accomplishing goals. I did the work, literally. In fact, I understand what Life Coach and Minister Iyanla Vanzant means when she advises people that desire to get their lives together. I always hear her say on her television broadcast you can get your life together but, "You have to do the work!" I appreciate this advice to the tenth power!!

Personally, in many ways I am still "doing the work" and this is fine because for me it's no cliché – doing the work is continual. And, even when I reach my main goal and dreams I must dream a new dream. Or, until I reach excellence in every area of my life I must "do the work". Excellence for me advocates the pursuit of perfecting well-intended goals and executing the work and action toward obtaining them.

Self-improvement should be the goal of everyone unless you're perfect and only Jesus Christ is the only known perfect man to ever walk the earth. Gandhi, Mother Teresa and maybe Buddha are close seconds. My point is that if we all have mindsets towards self-improvement on a consistent basis we understand that regularly aiming to self-improve isn't exclusively for those that need extra help to get their life back on track. The desire for progression is ageless. The need for rewarding oneself is a necessity. Let's not turn this into another way to become more selfish. Instead, let's simply reward ourselves as needed and hopefully prevent burnout in the process.

Working adults over twenty-one, how about that adventure? Something new? Perhaps skydiving? This is something I plan to experience in my lifetime. Not that adventurous? How about taking a local helicopter ride? It might bring joy to your overworked life. It might also be liberating to experience something different and new. You may relieve some stress in the process of rewarding yourself. Choosing to have wholesome fun is not a crime. Never rewarding yourself for all you do should be a crime.

Make time to do whatever your pleasure may be. (This assumes your pleasure is something legal that does not cause harm to others.) Many work hard for comfort but never have an ample amount of time to enjoy the comforts they've worked so hard for. They feel empty inside or they burnout easily. Perhaps they saw to everyone else's needs except their own. Well you now have permission to be good to yourself – reward yourself without feeling guilty. I insist that you don't spend another minute ignoring you. Okay?

# Chapter

# *Twelve*

## Help Is Available

*I*t doesn't matter who you are or how successful you may be everybody needs help at some time or another in life; it doesn't cease after you become a full-fledged adult either. I venture to say that there are at least five categories where humans need help: physical, mental, spiritual, emotional and/ or financial help. And of these five we have needed help in at least one of these categories at some point in our lives and you may be in a state of denial if you don't believe this.

Believe it or not many people suffer physically because they are afraid to seek medical attention. They feel as though they could somehow prevent the worst from happing if they stay as far away from a doctor or hospital as possible by refusing to hear or learn what the actual truth is about their health condition. I've been guilty of this behavior only to discover that I was being foolish. Thankfully, it was nothing too serious and I'll never make that mistake again and neither should you.

Mental health is a subject that I should not entertain because my views are strict and might be perceived as being cold. It's my understanding that mental health challenges is due to a chemical imbalance, which is something that I agree with; however, I also believe there are milder cases of mental issues that are more emotional than clinical. This is where we should agree to disagree with each other's viewpoints.

Some matters are undeniably causes for emotional discomfort such as, grief over a deceased loved one, the unexpected loss of a job/career, an incurable disease to oneself or a loved one, or divorce. These are areas that we may not have any control over and heaven forbid if this is the case due to the fact that it could leave us in the worst case of being distraught. My prayer is that you solicit help via a reputable clergy person or certified therapist if this describes your current situation. Most states have free clinics for those that qualify. If you cannot afford therapy and are not eligible to receive free services you should talk to a qualified ordained pastor, chaplain, or seminary trained ministers that have a counseling background. Most clergy people who pastor a church don't charge a fee to their members for services rendered. And, they are usually qualified to recommend help if one's problem is beyond their counseling abilities.

As you may have already ascertained the spiritual area can be likened to seeking help from a clergy person. Don't be too quick to spew negativity about clergy people; we are not all bad – we just happen to be as human as you are. This doesn't excuse improper behavior of clergy folks that we hear about in the news; this simply suggest that we should not lump all clergy people into the hostility department because of a few rotten apples. Clergy people should have a higher standard in their behavior. To discredit all clergy would be just like saying all blondes are dumb and we know that is not true! It would also be like saying all brunettes are intelligent, which likewise isn't true. One doesn't have to be blonde, brunette, etc. to be considered intelligent or less than intelligent. After all is said, seek quality recommendations and trust your instincts if you decide to confide in a cleric or a professional therapist. Either of these could make a positive impact to your life.

Another category is financial help; not everyone falls into this category. Maybe you were born wealthy, if not; maybe you learned from youth how to effectively manage money. Either way, you should be grateful if this category does not apply to you. Consider helping someone else get back on track and know that helping does not have to translate into giving away all of your money. I had a friend who was forced to live on her on at an early age but she didn't have a clue about how to budget money. One of her colleagues sat with her and taught her how to budget her rent, utility bills, groceries and day-to-day living (food, transportation to and from work). This friend was actually better at budgeting money in her late teens than she was in her thirties. Go figure. At least she did well for herself when she was in dire straits.

Even though it's okay to help others by giving them money you should only give what you can comfortably afford. In other words, don't go broke giving away your money. In fact, if you follow Christian beliefs you know that God expects you to be a good steward over His money, which just happens to be in your possession, see Luke 16 of the Bible.

It's one thing to occasionally help someone out every once in a while; but it's another thing to become an enabler. Why should they be careful with their money since they know they always have access to yours? A responsible borrower may not feel this way and will make it their mission in life to return borrowed money and also better manage their money.

Conversely, an irresponsible person that frequently borrows will not try to be financially responsible and live within their own means – they will milk you forever IF you allow it.

Lending out money is something altogether different and we must apply wisdom whenever lending lest you risk never getting it back. Please be clear if you give others a loan and tell them to state the exact date they plan to pay you back; in fact, get it in writing if the amount is more than five dollars. If the person takes offense and refuses to sign the pay-back agreement maybe they had an ill-intended motive. You shouldn't lend money to that person. Neither should one lend to a person that habitually asks for money – it could be that they don't know how to manage money, which is not your problem.

If you are super spiritual and believe God told you to lend out the money he placed in your care you should yield to God and keep in mind that God will not tell you to do anything contrary to what's in Scripture. Neither should you grumble if it takes a well-intended borrower longer than expected to repay you. This assumes your lifestyle won't be effected if repayment comes later rather than sooner. You still should not get attitudinal even if the debt effects your budget, because the super spiritual understands that God is looking more at your reaction and character regarding the loan than he is the borrower, who may have an acceptable reason for the delay. Besides, maybe you are not as super spiritual as you think you are if considering all the blessings that you possess, you decide to forget about trusting the One who provided all your blessings in the first place.

Furthermore, don't blame me if you take this advice and it goes south – take it up with God since you believe he told you to give the at-risk loan. It is okay to lend; just do it in wisdom and trust that you'll be better than okay whether or not the borrower repays you. Again, this assumes you lent within your comfortable means.

As stated earlier there are many methods of helping others. Helping could be sharing information about how to prepare and stick to a budget or sharing other beneficial financial tips. We must apply wisdom in all our interactions because at the end of the day we must be able to live with our choices as opposed to stressing over our choices.

Personally, I've learned the hard way about being overly generous with money. This doesn't mean that I've become hardened about helping; it just means I pray and think on it beforehand.

My other "she-ro" is my favorite aunt. She is a retired widower, raised two sons (by herself) that are doing well for themselves, lives on a fixed income and does very well for herself. And she is also a senior citizen that is in the best physical health. I have much love and admiration for her mostly because I've known her my entire life and appreciate how independent she is.

I don't recall exactly when my aunt and I had the conversation regarding borrowing or lending money. Our relationship is such that it's nothing for us to be on the phone for two hours in one setting mostly because that's how we often visit – via the telephone. I shared with her how upset I was because years ago I'd allowed a friend to borrow money but the person dodged me when it was repayment time. I vented how I always got the short end of the stick for trying to do good deeds. She listened patiently and added that she made it a rule to never lend out money.

My report was better by our next conversation. I affirmed how I demanded the person to pay me back and how they eventually complied (this was way before I became spiritually mature). It was at this point my aunt asserted that she never lends money. She reasoned that if she could budget well on a fixed income, therefore others who work fulltime should be able to maintain way better than her and that they do not need her money. Playing advocate, I asked what happens if she was ever short and required a loan. Her humorous response was something like, "I borrow from my friends Visa and Master Card whenever I fall short!" This made me laugh out loud. My aunt has always lived within her means, which is something that many of us, for whatever reason, don't do.

While I'm not as strict as my aunt I certainly understand why she's taken this position when it comes to finances. Being widowed early in life she had to learn how to be fiscally responsible especially since she had two sons to raise on her own, which by the way, she did an excellent job. Both my cousins are doing well. What's even more admirable is that she never stepped foot inside anyone's college (except maybe attend her sons' graduations) yet she manages money extremely well, you'd think she had a Ph.D. in Money Management but she doesn't! She simply learned how to handle and respect money. I would also venture to say that she was good at money-management way before she became a widow. Being widowed merely intensified someone whose skills were already on point.

What does this have to do with age? Everything. If you learn how to properly manage money before or during your teen years, it's safe to believe you will be financially responsible by the time you become an adult. It is not unusual to carry childhood habits into your adult life including in the area of managing money.

Many adults kick themselves because they did not handle their money properly and now live from paycheck to paycheck. They want to take a cruise or another fabulous vacation but are too financially strapped. This is not a fun position to be in; even if you don't care about traveling you care about something that requires money. Maybe it's driving a nice car or maybe you're a fashionista and enjoy shopping; but wouldn't it be a shame if you can't either drive a nice car or shop until you drop all because you mishandled your money in the early years or accumulated a ton of debt? It's not worth it. Plan well and save yourself some possible grief by doing right by your finances at every age.

# PART III

## Live Life To The Full!

# Chapter

# Thirteen

## Embrace the Aging Process

Aging, without a doubt, is inevitable; so why not embrace the process? There's nothing you can do to prohibit the cycle of age. Sure, you can slow down the process by being good to your body. Or you can augment this and Botox that to alter your appearance to make yourself look younger; and no judgment here if that's your thing. The bottom line is underneath it all we still age and we don't have to be anxious about it.

If you haven't guessed by now I'm obsessed with age, but in a positive way. My inspiration regarding the conversation regarding age started with listening to others blame age for many things such as not completing their education, not going for better jobs/careers and I've also met people who blamed age for not relocating or purchasing property. The story almost always begins, "I'm too old now...maybe if I were younger I could..." Stop it! Poor health may be a valid reason why you cannot do this or that; but not your age. In reality it's never too late until you are dead!!

As alluded to in chapter four everything in creation ages. Many items get better with age; wine comes to mind...so I'm told, tee hee hee.

As people, like a vintage bottle of wine, we should also get better with age. We should be wiser, fruitful and better understand what's truly important in life. Wisdom suggests we understand it's not all about us and it doesn't matter how much or how little you have; one way or another you're dependent on others for survival. If you don't agree with this then you just don't know!

Fruitfulness has to do with whom and where you allocate the majority of your time. Your allocation of time has to do with what you most value. If you work nonstop although you can live well without overworking, perhaps you value money over free time.

You may need a hobby if you watch television all day and half the night purely for the sake of entertainment and nothing else. Same goes for Facebook. I rarely visit Facebook more than a few minutes a day. If I'm on it longer than increments of ten minutes it's because I haven't checked it in a few weeks and spend extra time catching up. I hear about people that seem to be on it morning, noon, and night and wonder where they get the time. Some people seem so obsessed with social media it also makes me wonder if they have real live relationships. Again, no judgment, just pointing out what we value. Truthfully, I'd rather see people obsessed with social media as opposed to messing up other people's lives (and hopefully they are not messing up other people's lives through social media bullying).

What's truly significant in life is how we treat others; it's definitely one of the top three important things in life. This doesn't mean we must view everyone as our best friend. Instead this assumes that if we simply respect others, no matter how we feel inside, the world would be a better place if we were at least cordial to one another. If age should not be a deterrent for reaching goals in life; neither should it be a deterrent in how we treat others.

The aging process goes beyond aging chronologically. We age in wisdom, developmentally, experientially and/or spiritually to name a few. I won't go into great detail about aging in wisdom except to say that wisdom is not the same as being intelligent. Food for thought: intelligence can be knowing that a tomato is a fruit, whereas wisdom knows not to put a tomato into a fruit salad. One can possess a ton of intelligence but still be lacking in wisdom.

An acquaintance of mine married a successful doctor, had children, new car, new SUV and lived in a beautiful home. She marveled about being relieved to be a stay-at-home mom, which is something that I can personally relate. She discussed how she frequently asked her husband if they could comfortably afford all of the comforts they enjoyed and confessed his response to her was simply to sit back and let him handle the finances. Her only job was to be a wife and mother. They had a custom-made home, custom-made furniture and expensive artwork, no prints! Unfortunately, she had to return to work when their children became school aged because her doctor husband had to file for bankruptcy. He earned a handsome salary but overspent. I was in shock because I naively thought it was impossible for people that earned a six-figure plus income to go broke, or worse – deep debt to the point of bankruptcy. I felt so bad for her because I was a stay-at-home mom and was grateful not to have to depend on babysitters. (I would have gladly babysat for her free of charge but we did not live in the same city.)

We see in this example that although one was intelligent enough to become a certified medical doctor he was not as wise in his money-managing skills. I've seen less educated people do a much better job of managing their money. And, I don't share this to poke fun – it would be as if the kettle calling the pot black. It's true. I was not a genius in handling my own financial affairs and learned the hard way to do better. My point is that for whatever reason mishandling money had more to do with lack of wisdom or restraint but not intelligence.

We mature as we age chronologically…at least we should. Some are forced to mature quickly. Maybe they are forced to grow up too fast due to irresponsible parents. I've seen cases where a single parent overloaded the eldest child with responsibilities that no child should have. Children should be free to be children without having adult responsibilities. This doesn't mean that children shouldn't have chores; it means that children should be able to play when other kids are playing instead of doing adult chores.

You may argue that this scenario helps the overworked child to become more responsible later in life; but I respectfully disagree in that while they might become more responsible, more often than not that child lacks in personality or takes life too seriously. Some of them miss out on having a normal childhood, then later try to recapture their childhood by reverting back to childhood behavior at a time when they're supposed to be mature adults.

Worse is when these children who are now adults that have grown up to become impossible to deal with due to the fact that they're too serious and never learned how to relax. I don't believe we should be in a perpetual state of idiocy or play too much; yet there should be a nice balance of seriousness and hilarity. Excessiveness in either direction may not benefit anyone.

Another manner of aging is through our experiences or we can say that we age experientially. One fascination I had when

I was a seminarian was learning the connotations of theological terminology. I possess a love for words and was thrilled when required to learn new words – most of which I never knew before my course of study. By the way, all theological terms are not confined to theology, it was through studying in a systematic and structured setting where most theological terms were introduced to me. Of all the numerous terms I learned there are at least three that are forever embedded in my memory: a posteriori, priori and hermeneutics. As just mentioned, all of these terms do not have to exclusively be considered theological terms yet it was during my tenure as a theology student when I discovered them. Some terms may overlap in other subjects such as philosophy.

If memory serves me correctly the term *a priori* suggests something that is assumed without reference to actual experience; unlike *a posteriori* which refers to a reasoning or an assertion that is dependent on an actual experience and is not assumed. Theologically speaking, if one observes creation, that is, trees, flowers, animals and sees in it an organized pattern, it might be concluded as being a posteriori, such as on the basis of observing creation that God exists as the creator of nature. However, if God's existence can be proved on some basis prior to experience, then the existence of God can be argued an a priori or theory.

For many, experience is the best teacher. I think about my sons during their early college years. It didn't matter how much advice I gave they always learned their biggest lessons via personal experience that were contrary to my advice. In their defense, I guess I was a lot like them at that age. The biggest difference is I wasn't afforded the same freedom to study my areas of interest when I was their age.

My oldest son went to school on the west coast and required a car for transportation. My husband and I literally begged him not to purchase a new car while pursuing a BA because of the financial burden it would create for him. We offered to fix up our 1994 Maximum, which still runs perfectly by the way, and ship it to him from Chicago – but noooooo, he had to have a new car. We expressed that we could not afford car payments and he decided to work to pay for it himself. Nine months in, the new car novelty wore off and he confessed he wished he had waited. I felt bad for him and truly would have picked up the financial slack if I could have at that time. The reality is that he needed to learn that lesson for himself.

My youngest son is not above reproach either. I literally begged him to get his driver's license before he left for college but he didn't listen and to this day Uber is making a small fortune off him because of it (he finally got his driver's license). He's home on a break from college and worked downtown. He called me one day at the end of his shift for me to come pick him up. Turns out it was only 9 P.M. but I was tired and had already turned in for the night. My husband was also in for the night, which meant that my son had to take the L train home. He was annoyed because he hates taking public transportation, that is, buses or trains, after dark. Although he didn't have his license at that time, my husband and I would have helped him get a used car assuming he was a safe driver.

Once again, some of us insist on learning by way of experience. It's how we develop and grow; yet it could be useful to learn from the voice of other people's experience too, which could prevent setbacks and headaches. We know the saying, "experience is the best teacher" well I have a new saying: "just listen to the voice of reason and take its suggestions to avoid headaches".

This brings me to the discussion of spiritual aging. Spirituality is not the same as religion in my opinion so please read further instead of zoning out, okay? Spirituality has to do with being in tuned with oneself and one's intuition. It has the potential to be totally focused if we listen and allow ourselves to be led by that still small voice within us. We can test ourselves by trusting that small inner voice one time to see if we can trust it; I believe we can trust it and if our spirituality comes through for us once then it most certainly can lead us to the passage of restoration, reflection, peace and general contentment for our lives and hearts. You might say I'm having a serious "Kumbaya" moment and that's okay. I love the Kumbaya song and don't care that people have become cynical about its representation. In a casual discussion, my history buff friends shared, "Kumbaya, My Lord" was first recorded around 1927 by an unemployed literature professor, who searched for black spirituals and ultimately recorded a song entitled 'Come by Here, My Lord.' The song was sung in a language called Gullah that originated on some of South Carolina's islands. However, Gullah is a creole language; therefore, 'Come by here, my Lord' is Gullah for 'Kum by (h)yuh, my lawd'.

"'Kumbaya' became a practical song of choice with American Boy Scouts and Girl Scouts during bonfires at camp sites. The mood of the campers was harmonious and serene, yet cynics throughout the US changed this harmless word into something as being too squeaky clean or unrealistic."

It's a shame that we've either become too sophisticated, insensitive, or cold to appreciate something this innocent. I bet the view of the populace regarding "Kumbaya" would be more favorable and accepting if Jay Z, an American rap artist, were to rap "Kumbaya" in one of his songs. I say this because I believe Jay Z can make most anything sound cool. Moreover, sometimes society can be impulsive by quickly jumping on the bandwagon by flowing with the tide of popularity if they believe they're somehow cooler by going with the majority. They quickly change courses about what was previously considered uncool or out of touch. So much for personal integrity...

We don't have to act holier than thou or be super holy in order to mature spiritually or for some, innately possess spiritual maturity. It's acceptable to have a "Kumbaya" attitude without acting like a Pharisee, which were biblical hypocrites. Aging spiritually lends itself to having inner beauty that outwardly manifests. There are many more elements to spiritual aging but let's first get the basics down packed. Evidence of the spiritually mature is manifold; yet a fundamental evidence could be the type of character one possesses and attract. The spiritually aged individual also has an inner peace. This inner peace is evident in the midst of personal storms as well, which is also a testament of one's character and integrity.

I love all types of people. This doesn't purport that I agree with wrongdoings because I don't. Neither do I believe I'm better than anybody because of my affections for all people – this simply means people intrigue me and also that I've grown in my personal spirituality that enables me to see good in most people.

Please don't misunderstand me. I don't love Hitler or other murderers like him. It means that I try to love who God loves and hate what and who God hates...if such a thing is possible. It also means that I've learned how to love unconditionally. In fact, I tend to better get along with others that give me the freedom to be me, flaws included.

It's one of the many reasons why I love my husband so much. I've never met a man who totally accepts me for who I am. I was comfortable with him from the time we met over twenty years ago until now. Is our relationship perfect? Hecky no!!! It means that I'm free to be me without being punished for it.

My best friend in the world is old enough to be my mother. Everyone calls her Aunt Bootsie. I've known her longer than my husband and she likewise loves me for me – flaws and all. Through the years many have tried to discourage our friendship but our friendship has stood the test of time. We met at my second real job out of high school. Our offices were next door to each other. She was so nice to me that I thought she was gay and later learned she wasn't and actually had a husband. It was my first day at work, I had the worst monthly cramps and Bootsie brought me some hot tea. No one had been as accommodating to me and trust me, I am an approachable person. Our friendship developed and I love her like a mother.

Some peers once told me that she spoke negatively about me behind my back. This angered me because the very gossips that shared this information with me always gossiped about everyone on the planet. There's no way I would ever believe this mostly because even if there was a shred of truth to what they said, which it wasn't, there was no way I would have ignored all the good she had done for me. She spoiled me; I was the daughter she never had. She never understood why the relationship I had with my own mother was strained. My own mother and I basically got along but as mother-daughter relationships go we went through an awkward phase (I thank God we reconciled before she died).

One of Bootsie's friends likewise tried to interfere with our friendship. Although I was barely out of high school I had my own studio apartment and used to spend a lot of time at her house. Her friend told her she was a fool for having this young girl around her husband so frequently but Bootsie is neither the jealous type nor insecure and kept me around since forever.

My grandmother loved and appreciated her too; she saw how kind she was to me and warned me to keep her as a friend, which is exactly what I did and we remain friends today some twenty-five plus years later.

The take away here can also be not to allow age to prohibit or deter friendships. One of many commonalities Bootsie and I have is our love for all people. Sure, we talk about people but always in a fun-loving manner. Her sense of humor is that of a comedian; in fact, we (my friends and I) always tell her that she missed her calling and would be the funniest comedienne. She relays real live stories and make you laugh until you cry. You have to be present to know what I'm talking about, but to know her is to love her.

Society weighs heavily on views about age and will lead you to believe that youth is all the rage. Maybe this is true? Maybe not so much? Youth for the most part is undeniably pretty but we know it takes more than looks to survive; and even if one is fortunate enough to make it solely based on looks we know it's temporary; looks change. Things and people age; this is not a bad thing but it is the truth.

We mustn't be negatively swayed by societal views. Rather we should learn how to extract what works to our benefit. Opinions are like noses: everybody has one. It isn't until we walk into our own integrity with consideration that we thrive; and once we thrive we are better positioned to help others thrive. This is what life should be about: helping one another for the common good.

It might be my imagination but it seems as though we live in an extremely selfish society where connection to people seem to decrease by leaps and bounds. Many may have an inner circle of friends but even within inner circles there seems to be a measure of exclusion. Maybe it's due to the diversity of beliefs. I don't judge it; I observe it and if these observations are accurate how can we progress as people? Maybe I'm overthinking it. Yet, you can be in my inner circle even if your thoughts flow differently than mine. What's the problem if we relate respectfully to one another? How can we prohibit age or status from interfering with what is most important? Which is to be kind to everyone.

I'm in the opinion that the action of one person has great potential. Positive actions of one attracts one more then before you know it an entire group is birthed in positivity. I observe the homosexual community and how organize they are or seem to be. Not to take away from any other group but truthfully, there was a time in US history where homosexuality was closeted and that was the end of the story. Nowadays homosexual marriage is legal in many states and if I were a betting woman I'd say it started with one dedicated person and multiplied into a community of people that boldly stood for something they collectively agree upon. Note: I'm not offering any views regarding homosexuality. It's my observation and I call it the way I see it.

I observe groups that protect animals. These people are passionate and make a difference in the life of pets that were mistreated or neglected by humans. They organize and create adoption agencies that place pets in loving households. Helping pets is great. How much greater would it be if that same passionate energy was put into homelessness? Of hungry children? Of orphans?

Or, has that same energy been put into homelessness or human orphans and we have not heard about the positive results? Positive reports have the potential to create more positive actions towards getting all involved in helping the homeless, hunger and orphans. It would be great to hear massive reports regarding a possible worldwide end to homelessness, hunger, orphans and also modern-day slavery/white slavery.

Or does it stand to reason that we've become too cold to care about others we might view as being less than? Do we use our age as an excuse not to care? The so-called restriction of age with respect to reaching personal goals and personal development goes beyond the individual in that it has the potential to affect others and possibly society. So, it's never too late to do your part to help others from where you are and you do not have to be rich to help others.

Too many times we tell ourselves that we have to get it together before we attempt to do something for someone or some other cause. I submit that if you could get yourself together you would have already done it; therefore, stop the delay by stepping outside of your comfort zone and do something worthwhile for someone else. One four-hour shift at a homeless shelter could make a world of difference. Still too much? Then, how about one two-hour shift twice a week. Maybe commit to cleaning up or emptying the garbage, which may actually take less time to do.

Financial support to a reputable ministry could positively change a third world life. Helping a senior citizen that lives alone could earn an extra star on your crown. Maybe the senior needs something from the grocery store or pharmacist, or just desires company, but you won't know unless you become vulnerable by offering to help. These are only a few suggestions. Deep down inside you know there is something constructive that you can do besides shop for yourself. You can share your daily Starbucks with someone who can't afford it by buying two ventis instead of the grandé you usually get for yourself. What about all the movies and other activities of entertainment you treat yourself to? There's nothing wrong with participating in these after all, you've worked all week long and deserve a weekend outlet. What about extending help to others less fortunate than you? You could very well extend yourself by helping others. It's also my belief that it can take our focus off whatever personal issue we may have if we redirect our focus by helping someone else.

Maybe society has you stuck in your rut because you believe its hype. I've viewed television programs that tell you what fashion to wear, what works and what doesn't work. It amuses me how people frequently forgo their personal likes and adjust by wearing what's mandated by society. It's okay to enjoy wearing the latest fashion trends. I also enjoy fashion as much as the next person because there's no harm in it. The harm comes when you purchase something that you cannot afford solely because of the designer label. That's beyond my comprehension! Especially if you cannot afford lunch until your next pay period.

I know women that fall victim to expensive hair extensions when they know they don't actually have the budget for it. I used to be in this category but not anymore. The inner guilt ate me alive because I'm usually practical in my spending habits. There's nothing wrong with being fashionable or wearing hair extensions; in fact, many of us look fabulous in our extension hairdo. Please don't misunderstand me. I enjoy seeing women who take pride in their appearance from fashion to hair extensions. My point from the beginning is to encourage you to challenge yourself and go beyond the ordinary. My goal is also to encourage you to consider a broader mindset mostly because sooner or later we learn that there is no real fulfillment in fashion, expensive hairdos or materialism solely for the purpose of having stuff. There is fulfillment in things that go beyond outward appearance that can positively be impactful without going broke. Please trust me on this. Also note this doesn't apply to women who are already established in their careers and can comfortably afford to keep up with the latest trends.

Aging is a peculiar thing to me. I witness the changes in my body. I feel the difference in my level of energy compared to twenty years ago. Don't get me started on my graying hair, which by the way started when I was twenty-five. Actually, I was ten when I noticed my very first gray hair as were my two sons. Graying at ten was fun, we laughed about it. Graying at twenty-five was intriguing at first but more gray came at twenty-seven and this concerned me. I wasn't ready to invest in Dark'n Lovely dye yet, but it was fast approaching the time for me to start coloring my hair. The good news is sometimes I color it and sometimes I go au natural. I guess it depends on my temperament at any given moment.

Friends would tell me to leave it alone and said they wished they had gray, which was something I never understood. Who could want premature graying? I was regularly dying my hair by the time I was thirty-two! I was inwardly outraged and self-conscious but I had absolutely no control over how quickly the gray came so I redirected myself to working out. It's true; my exercise regimen was on point because I reasoned if I were going to look old my body was going to look young!

I was wrong on all accounts. One of the secrets of life is to enjoy your life exactly where you are at your current age. I'm not saying if you have life threatening issues to enjoy those. What I am conveying is how important it is to enjoy life without wanting to be a different age than you currently are.

I recall my oldest son couldn't wait until he was sixteen so that he could get his driver's license. I teased him by telling him it was a moot point because we couldn't afford car insurance for a teen. He quickly deflated and I quickly told him I was only kidding. He asked why I would do something like that. It was a fair question. I expressed to him that he should not put life on hold just because he did not yet have his license. I continued and said there will always be an age eligibility for something and he mustn't start off his young life by waiting; he must simply enjoy life exactly where he presently is. I shared how after he got his license he'd have to wait another two years to vote; and another three years to drink, another year if he desired to get married and forty to fifty years to retire. Do you really want to waste time waiting for the next thing? I think not!! Waiting for the next age can prohibit one from enjoying their current age.

My son responded and said he'd never thought about it like that and calmed down for about thirty seconds. It's in his nature to rush; but nowadays he understands the significance of slowing down a tad. To my surprise, he admitted this to me.

My younger son told me about two years ago that he likes having the safety net called parents. He said he's going to milk us for as long as we let him and he ain't never lied! Several friends asked him to get an apartment together as soon as he got a fulltime job, but he refused to move out at the time. He said he likes having free rent with his parents. My husband and I have set a deadline for him to move out lest we become enablers. We are currently empty nesters. Yay!

Our younger son was too hard on himself; I've frequently explained to him to stop looking at where others are in life and instead focus on his own life. He had some serious bumps along the way and is extremely unforgiving towards himself. Hopefully he will take responsibility for his choices and make wiser choices. I'm rooting for him. He's extremely talented but he doesn't seem to understand the depths of his talents. My advice to him is to always be ready because one never knows when opportunity will strike. I believe one big break could forever positively change his life; he only has to be ready.

I live in Chicago and there's no place I'd rather be during the summertime. I'm in the process of repairing the bikes at my disposal so I can ride to the lakefront and Navy Pier. My husband and sons never ride so I usually use their bikes except all are in need of repair. I'm actually thinking about purchasing my very own bike that has a basket for Tinéy, my Shih Tzu, so we can catch the lakefront breezes that I enjoy. Although I enjoy going to nice restaurants, shopping and many other types of entertainment I also enjoy time to myself just to read, meditate, journal and think about what new thing I can do to bless someone else. Not to brag but I donate a lot of time volunteering at nonprofits organizations and enjoy every minute of it.

In fact, for the first time in my life I was a bell-ringer for the Salvation Army a couple of winters ago. The weather was colder than a witch's tit but it was so much fun! I stood outside of Macey's on State Street and opened doors for shoppers. Many of them gave on their way out and stated they had no intentions of giving but gave since I held the door open for them. Many others thanked me for my service. It felt so good! Honestly!! I volunteered this past winter but unfortunately it wasn't the same experience, mostly because I only had time to ring for a couple of hours. It's my understanding that they pay their ringers except I never except pay because whatever monies I stand to earn as a ringer would go to a worthier cause to help others. This may not be your thing but you never know unless you try it. I hate cold weather, but what better way to deal with it than taking the focus off myself for a worthy cause. I'm not pushing this organization on you I'm only suggesting that you consider doing something out of the ordinary that will help someone else. As for me, I've already told the envoy that I will commit to bell ringing in the future.

I'm no do-gooder and have many flaws. Like the rest of us I am a work in progress and still have a long way to go. I'm not pretentious; neither am I above the law. What I am is one person who desperately want self-improvement and more importantly I desperately want to encourage others to become their best selves.

I'm reminded of my great-aunt who is ninety-eight years young! She was born in 1920. She is a riot and still parties. You heard me – she still gets her party on. She goes to casino boats, plays bidwhiz, keno and bingo. She finally visited my place of worship after a few invitations. I asked our gatekeeper, so to speak, to be on the lookout for her because she traveled via Pace, which is a bus service for senior citizens that qualify in Chicago. The bus pulled up just as I went to look for her a few minutes before Service started. I greeted, kissed and welcome her then excused myself to go to the Ladies' Room one last time before the service got underway. To my surprise, she was still talking to our gatekeeper. I heard her say, "Where you been all my life?" and teased her mercilessly afterwards by saying it took numerous invitations for me to get her to a holy place but it only took her two seconds to get her flirt on, lol. She insisted that he'd said it first and she only repeated it back to him. I said, "Sure, uhm huh, that's your story and you're sticking to it."

She and I tease each other in laughter all the time. She confessed that she had a good time and plans to return for another visit, except my assignment at that church has ended. My girlfriends and I always say that we want to be like Aunty when we become seniors. People love her and also love her sense of humor. She still enjoys life at ninety-eight.

Please enjoy your life at the age you presently are. Life is beautiful; but if we waste time focusing on what's wrong in our lives instead of what's right then life will pass by us. Although we live in certain environments where the media and society has the potential to affect the way we think we must not allow negative influences control our mindsets. This may sound challenging at the onset but in actuality this does not have to be a challenge and what we must do to combat impending negativity is be determined to stand in our own integrity for our own betterment, which also includes going outside ourselves in positivity with a goal of being an asset in life and towards others. A little bit of growth can go a long way but it starts with movement. Let's go from stagnation or potential growth to actual kinetic growth keeping in mind that our movement does not have to be grandiose; it must simply be positive, effective, well-intentioned and honest. Our little growth can start off small, develop, then eventually become grandiose.

# Fourteen

## What the Heck Does This Side of 40 Mean Anyway?

*E*arlier I mentioned that the aging process intrigues me. One reason is because we enter the world totally tiny, innocent and dependent on someone to care for us. We develop, learn, make choices and go through trials and triumphs. If we're lucky (not that I believe in luck) our loved ones capture significant moments of our lives or simply snap pictures and videos for keepsakes. Before age ten we already hear talk of how quickly we've grown up.

Our outward appearance changes as we physically develop. Boys and girls alike experience adolescent development also known as growing pains. Around age eleven boys' voices begin to deepen; and girls' boobies begin to hurt as they begin to fill those beginner's brassieres. What seems like centuries later I still recall that pain and wonder why did it have to hurt so much?! These takes place before either gender barely enters the double digits.

The teen years arrive and more challenges in life for teens and parents alike arrive. Even those that don't have children hear about the stories of peer pressure, academic highlights and lowlights, teen pregnancies, teen drug use, teen sports' victories and everything in between.

One day my baby was a girl and the next day she's a woman. Same with the guys; one day they mimic dad shaving and the next day their shaving off their own facial hair. It's how it is in aging – seemingly nonstop progressive.

Some go away to college after high school, some take up a trade, some do both, or decide to only work or join the military. Many are fortunate and get that dream job immediately after graduating college. Others know affluent people, a friend of the family, or join their family owned enterprise. It doesn't matter how good or bad they are they'll never get fired due to the strong network of their professional connection. Some other company schmuck is required to go behind the newly hired wannabee executive to make sure the recent grad doesn't mishandle important company business. The fresh out of college grad in reality will never learn the corporate ropes or be effective in their newfound position unless a higher up demands it. This scenario isn't always the case. There are responsible grads that go out of their way to be great at their careers even the careers that were handed to them on a sliver patter.

There's another percentage of young adults that do nothing but play video games and maybe smoke blunts, drink alcohol, or both. Another percentage break into the homes of people that work hard for a living. Some join street gangs. It's an awful truth that started with one's choice. Some may not know why they make unwise choices or don't care; perhaps they don't see their choices as unwise. Others make right choices but their hearts aren't in it and they have zero passion about choices made. Maybe they decided to appease their parents or worse: perhaps they got caught up in a desperate situation that they felt was hopeless, which therefore, caused them to make a choice they might not have otherwise made, which was due to fear. It doesn't take long for them to become stuck; at least that's the lie they believe. So many accept being stuck in various adverse situations. Some are in a type of emotional or financial dependence as a way of life at practically any age. Feeling stuck is bondage and I encourage you to reread chapter one then afterwards please be determined to figure it out. I don't claim that it will be easy but one thing I know for certain is that no good thing will happen if your potential energy isn't propelled into kinetic energy. This is for sure!

We find ourselves as full-fledged adults with adult responsibilities. We buy, cars, condos, homes and some of us start families of our own. Those of us that manage money well take fabulous vacations. Some of us take fabulous vacations that land us in debt. Some of us are too tired to take a vacation and prefer to just stay at home and relax, which is totally acceptable. Whatever the scenarios we keep plunging forward. For sure we keep aging.

Some choose to remain single. Some marry and stay married. Some marriages tragically end in divorce. Some remarry; some vow to never marry again. My step-grandfather once said that everyone should at least try it once. I don't know if I believe that especially for this era. I believe everyone should be honest about their feelings; and either accept or politely reject people for who they are in reference to relationships including marriage. This presumes rejection occurs before walking down the aisle of holy matrimony.

We're in our thirties and either love, hate, or feel indifferent about our jobs/careers. We know we have to work unless we've won the lottery. It's amazing to meet those that love what they do for their livelihood. It's sad to see people with stressful jobs. I know a couple of case managers and counselors that dream of retiring due to the stress that comes with the nature of their jobs. The same with inner city teachers and floor nurses. They used to love what they do until it become too dramatic in more ways than one.

Many adults over thirty-five return to school for a higher degree with the hope of landing that dream job or for sure landing a job that drastically increases their salary. I've met at least seven people over fifty that hate their current jobs and went back to school, completed their course of study, but have not gotten their dream job. Of the seven one is heartbroken and depressed, one is hopeful and one rolls with the tide hoping for her desired success but not obsessing over how things currently are. As for the others, I'm not sure how they feel to be in the same position except to declare it must be hard to complete a higher degree in one's field and not get the preferred career. To this I say figure out a way to create your own opportunity. We hear of numerous people that post on YouTube and get discovered…I'm just saying. You may not choose to go this route but you can figure out how to do your heart's desire and get paid for doing it. I have faith in you!

We live and become adults and when we become adults we're adults for the rest of our lives. We enjoy life or don't. We understand our purpose or don't. We accept our purpose or don't. We are content or not; I don't necessarily believe in happiness except to say it's temporary. I believe in contentment, which for me necessitates peace of mind. My peace of mind is everything! And, I'd walk a country mile for it. This doesn't mean that happiness for me is unwelcomed. Many people feel that happiness is or should be continuous; and if that's your thing more power to you. The issue I have with being in a perpetual state of happiness is that it's unrealistic. I'd rather have joy because unlike happiness joy can exist in the midst of a storm and is not codependent on circumstances. Besides, what would one do if he/she is suddenly thrust into an uncontrollable state of ongoing sadness or tragedy? Would he/she handle it or fall to pieces? There are those that feel comfortable in misery, which is mindboggling. Why spend your life being sad all the time? Who benefits from your permanent state of sadness? It doesn't make them right and me wrong; it's just one more ideation for consideration: is there anything productive about being sad all the time? Or always wallowing in self-pity?

Like it or not people, society, commercials, money-makers, or whatever, assist in shaping our perceptions regarding personal self-actualization. It's left up to the individual to be persuaded one way or the other. Aging is for sure one of life's constants. We can Botox it, dye it, or liposuction it away and it will not change the fact that aging is inevitable; yet how we treat the inevitability of aging is what counts. Entering a state of sadness as a lifestyle is tragic and has the ability to cause premature age lines that can negatively affect one's appearance.

Do we mistreat young girls and envy them for their youth? Do we hate that young guy that outshot us on the b-ball court? If you've answered yes to either you need help! On the other hand, if you interact with youthful people positively it may be a testament that you enjoyed your youth and welcome opportunities to help youngsters achieve and enjoy theirs as well.

When all is said *This Side of Forty* has a dual meaning: it means you're one day old to forty; and it also means you're forty and over. The latter technically means you're on *that* side of forty yet I specifically chose the age "forty" because I believe that everyone has multiple experiences by forty for sure, even those considered to be boring or uneventful have a measure of experience.

You may argue and say you know people that have truly lived by their twenty-fifth birthday. This would not be an argument for me – I'd glory in their spunk for being so vivacious! I enjoy people that know how to live it up as long as they don't bring harm to themselves or others.

There's an expression that says "life begins at forty" and I don't know who coined this phrase but I don't totally agree with it, even though I understand the cliché. Perhaps whoever coined it believed that it is impossible to have an adequate amount of wisdom until age forty. Or maybe they felt the societal hoopla that mandates we mustn't grow older gracefully but we should instead kick and scream each year lived after forty. Not me! I say enjoy every age you get!

Years ago, I had a conversation with a lady that used to do my hair. As we became better acquainted with each other she asked my age and I politely told her that I didn't disclose my age. I also told her it wasn't because I was embarrassed about my age and that it was merely something that for me is personal. She verbalized that I was indeed embarrassed otherwise I would share the info. I was quiet at that point and inwardly annoyed. She didn't even ask why; instead she jumped to a negative and inaccurate conclusion.

There were and still are reasons why I don't shout my age from to the rooftops. One reason is because my grandmother once told me that a woman that tells her age would tell anything and is unable to keep secrets. That stuck with me. I stopped telling my age after my twenty-second birthday but the hair stylist was clueless about that.

Another reason why I don't usually disclose my age is because for the longest I was self-conscious about not being where I felt I should be in life. I allowed normal expectations about where someone should be in life by a particular age guide my inner feelings which I now know is preposterous. I maintain that I am proud to be on *that* side of forty. Each day is a blessing and I don't mean this in a cliché kind of way but I now appreciate life to the depths of my being at every age.

I've suffered loss of loved ones as well as deep disappointments in general that have left me sleepless and melancholy. I've cried out to God Almighty and demanded that he change my circumstances. I've even blamed him during my early twenties for everything that was wrong in my life when the reality is that all I was and am is mostly based on the choices I've singlehandedly made. (I had sense enough to apologize to God through repentance.)

One constant that I'm proud of is no matter what happens I continue to love people, albeit some I have to love from afar. I even love folks that hate me. I frequently wonder how could anyone hate wonderful me. Back in a day I ran my mouth recklessly especially in retaliation or whenever I had to defend myself; however, did I deserve to be hated? I hope not. Hate is an emotion that will destroy the hater faster than the hated; so, my advice is to not hate. Figure out a method of reconciliation instead. Just a thought.

How do I feel about my current age? Great! Ideally, I would like to be in better shape and have perfect health but I'm good. Age and the aging process still intrigues me. It may be a natural progression but to me it remains a mystery.

This is silly but I wonder how it felt to be born an adult. Adam and Eve of the Bible come to mind. Let's accept for the sake of argument they were the first humans and not turn this into a controversy, okay? Adam was the first man and had no one else like himself. There were other life forms around – plants and animals, but nothing else like him existed until Eve was created. Can you imagine how he felt? Instant attraction and excitement I bet!

Eve receives a lot a flack. I use to accuse her of messing up eternal bliss due to sin. Maybe I was unfair, maybe not; yet I've wondered over and over what life would have been like if no one committed the first sin. Would we truly have appreciated the blissful paradise described in Scripture? Will we appreciate the promise of eternal bliss in the afterlife? This raises a whole other topic that I will not explore mostly because many that read this may already be angry that I keep bring up Christian influence even if they don't know with all certainty if I'm Christian. Can we all just get along? It seems ludicrous to hate someone because of their religious beliefs and/or influences. It would be better to try to proselytize them instead of hating them.

After giving thought to the first two people on the earth I now feel sorry for them. They had no point of reference except the obvious which was blind obedience that should have been enough but wasn't. The serpent was clever and tricked them and you know how the story ended. I couldn't stay upset with Eve because I had to ask myself how many times I have disobeyed my parents and authority and I had numerous points of reference unlike Adam and Eve who only had One Authority that she should have obeyed. Like me, Adam and Eve did however, foreknow the consequences for disobedience. It's possible they didn't know how severe the consequences they suffered would be until they experienced it. Sure, God told them the day they ate the fruit they would surely die but if you recall they did not drop dead on the spot for transgressing against God. They thought they would become more knowledgeable than God after they ate the fruit. They were wronger than two left shoes. Instead they were immediately kicked out of Eden and suffered true consequences. Previously they ran around the Garden stark naked and unashamed of their nakedness. Ignorance is bliss. Later they became harsh laborers in more than one way. The weight of sin fell on humanity from that point forward and this is why I feel sorry for them…to a degree. Adam lived over nine-hundred years. Imagine that? I wonder if he allowed his age or his sin to keep him from having joyful moments in life after sinning. (The account of Adam and Eve can be found in Genesis chapter 3. (KJV Bible)

I promised earlier that I'm not trying to convert you into becoming a born again anything and I hold to that. My goal from the beginning is to encourage you not to use *age* as a deterrent that keeps you from achieving goals and also to inspire you to consider mindsets that may be different from your typical manner of viewing situations. My prayer is that I've done my job well. My intentions are from my heart and stem from a place of love. Okay fine, burst out the violins.

You mean the world to me and I don't have to personally know you to feel this way. The fact that you are a human being is all I need to know. My other desire is for you to love yourself and learn from past mistakes as opposed to dwelling on them because if you/we dwell on past mistakes we can never grow.

If you think I have every material thing I want in life you are sorely mistaken; but this doesn't stop me from being content or from having unexplainable joy. What I have is people in my life that I love and they love me and this hasn't always been the case. There were times in my teens that I felt totally awkward and alone and felt as if the world was against me. I felt no one understood me let alone loved me. That was a dark time of my life but the good news is that even during that awkward phase I had an inner peace that was beyond my comprehension.

That time was so dark that I wished I had had the courage to kill myself. Forgive my blunt opinion on this topic but suicide is a defeatist offense, there's always a better solution other than suicide, even though I suspect there are some that don't share this view. Furthermore, suicide might incorrectly be viewed as selfishness due to the pain it leaves in the loved ones of suicide victims. Most family members and friends of a suicide victim simply cannot relate to why the victim didn't seek their help in order to find a better option instead of taking one's own life. We must find a way to affectively deal with things we cannot change and be determined to survive through the hard stuff by trusting that things will eventually get better. Admittedly, this takes courage. Please don't let anyone or any circumstance deny you the opportunity to live and enjoy your life. Nothing bad lasts forever; we just have to be patient and trust that time truly can improve whatever hardship we may be experiencing.

It's my understanding that traditionalists believe those that commit suicide automatically spend eternity in hell. Contrary to my bold views on the subject of suicide, I believe there are exceptions to the rule. For instance, I don't believe the Almighty will condemn the slaves that jumped off the boat to be freed from slavery to hades for all eternity. Those who were captured suffered brutality en route to America. Neither do I believe poor victims of bullying will suffer eternally. I was once a teen and I experienced social awkwardness and could barely take it; therefore, I cannot fathom how hard it is for an individual who's actually being brutally bullied in person or through social media. My desire is for victims to know beyond a shadow of a doubt that they absolutely can get through rough times; they need to express what they're going through to a reliable adult, which might help change their circumstances for the better. Please don't give bullies the satisfaction of taking your own life. You will not hurt that unscrupulous bully nowhere near as much as your parents, loved ones and friends who will greatly suffer as result of missing you. Bullies are mean; some are even heartless and may not be affected by your suicide at all.

Besides, we don't know with all certainty what's on the other side…what happens when we die, meaning that no one in this century has ever died, experience afterlife for several years and then came back to share exactly what we could look forward to in the afterlife. Remember the movie *Beetlejuice*? Without going into great detail, the teenage girl played by Wynona Ryder wanted to kill herself until this dead couple convinced her not to kill herself due to the fact that life after death wasn't any better but, in some ways, they pled that the other side was worse. I mention this to support why one should not consider doing something as final as suicide. One should at least seek wise counsel at the first thought of suicide.

Another point, I realize some may prefer suicide to some horrifically painful disease and may argue that it is easy for me to have strong opinions. If you feel this way, truly I understand your position. Personally, I believe in miracles and pray miracles for anyone who is suffering beyond his/her control.

To the religious zealots that know by faith what your destination is please don't make a big deal out of this because this writing doesn't convey my personal thoughts on the afterlife. Okay? You're entitled to your beliefs, which is fine by me; I, as well as others, am likewise entitled to my beliefs.

We know there's an uncountable amount of evil in the world. Thankfully there's also good; subsequently don't waste time or linger in the dark crevices of your mind. Instead, get out and join life; enjoy life without bringing someone else down. Refuse to be that person that's miserable and spreads misery to others. Treat yourself to some contentment. Although I believe happiness is temporary treat yourself to some happiness too!

Isn't any kind of happiness better than being miserable? Be determined to live your life in a long-lasting state of contentment.

I cannot begin to tell you how to conduct your life if you are imprisoned or worse, imprisoned for something you didn't do. One point I can make is that there are people that may not be behind bars but live in an imprisoned mind; and believe it or not, in some ways the incarcerated has more freedom behind bars than one that isn't behind bars but lives an imprisoned lifestyle. We can argue that one is better off than the other; however, people in American prisons are not homeless and it's my understanding they receive three meals daily and work. This isn't to glorify imprisonment; rather this offers perspective particularly to those that are wrongfully imprisoned.

Repeat offenders that return to prison know what lies ahead; perhaps if it were that terrible for them they would never return. Of course, you could argue they had no intentions of getting caught; or you can argue they couldn't make it on the outside and subconsciously decided to go back. My hope is that they have some way of occupying their time while inside without an abundance of despair. Maybe those that ponder how to help can become the pen pal to an inmate. Minors **DO NOT** contact inmates without parental consent.

The truth of the matter is that at least two types of imprisonment exists; one is physical incarceration and the other is the imprisonment of one's mind. I wished I had more positivity to offer the imprisoned whether he/she is incarcerated or has an imprisoned mind. The best I can offer is that there are people you may not know that regularly pray for you and I hope you discover a constructive way of coping in life. Hope springs eternal and it's important not to ever give up. I'm sure it isn't easy for you or your loved ones and I offer that you speak with your chaplain, consider spiritual guidance, or professional therapy.

# Fifteen

## Give Back...Even if You're Not Wealthy

One of the biggest misconceptions seems to be that one has to be wealthy or economically well-off to give back in order to make a significant difference to others. The other misconception is that one has to have an abundance of time to make a difference. Neither is true; what's most needed in order to make a positive difference in the life of another or to the world is COMMITMENT! We should first decide to commit then we decide which direction to take toward helping.

Sooner or later we discover life isn't only about us. Those of us that have our basic needs met – food, water, shelter and clothing have more than most comparatively speaking. Struggling poor people who live in third-world countries would love to have edible food and shelter regularly. The natural attitude might be, "I can't help anyone else because I need all the help I can get myself..." If this is our normal mindset we should immediately change it. It's where we go wrong; we need to understand that it isn't until we reach out to help that help or goodness is then returned back to us. This assumes we have pure motives for desiring to help in the first place.

I witness emptiness in many and the commonality they share is selfishness, stinginess, and lack of empathy. Many in this category fail to understand why they experience a certain emptiness and are unaware that their lack of concern for someone else besides themselves is what holds them back. They go to work every day and get by on the bare minimum of life. They have activities they enjoy but live in a perpetual state of hollowness and for many that are called out on their behavior they have ready excuses. Or they'll give a dollar to a cause which actually emotionally hurt them to donate. They'd rather spent five dollars on coffee or beer, which done in excess may be brutal on the body, instead of donating five or more dollars to an orphanage or another charity.

Many float through life in despair not recognizing how a tiny act as giving of oneself could alter one's course. There are too many ways we can make positive differences. We can do the following:

- Donate to cancer/medical research
- Donate to homeless shelters
- Volunteer at homeless shelters
- Financially support homeless shelter
- Become a hospital volunteer
- Volunteer for the Salvation Army
- Volunteer at parachurches or social service administrations
- Volunteer at the YMCA
- Volunteer for a ministry
- Become a missionary (in the States or abroad)
- Babysit for family and friends (free of charge)

- Visit the sick and shut-in
- Visit nursing homes (not all seniors in these facilities have family)
- Volunteer to help American Veterans
- Volunteer at an animal clinic or pound
- Join coalitions that represent human rights i.e., human trafficking, racial bigotry
- Join neighborhood watches to name a few.

We don't have to be so tight with our pockets! We have bills but come on, will it truly set you back at this point to help another worthy cause? It's okay to give sacrificially especially if we tell ourselves we'll give as soon as our finances improve. For some the finances never greatly improve so you might as well give now.

I was employed with the Alderwoods Group during the time Hurricane Katrina wreaked havoc on New Orleans and was impressed by how quickly companies and donors all over the US and world sent their support. Alderwoods created a donation process that allowed employees to have funds taken directly from their paychecks, which I thought was genius and convenient. No one of course was under obligation to donate but I honestly believe everyone donated and some were extra generous.

This is what truly knocked me over with a feather. My oldest son earned an academic scholarship and attended this fancy-smancy boarding school on the east coast, Brooks high school, located in North Andover, MA. My husband and I were there visiting during Parents' Weekend and I met this blond athletic kid I hadn't met before (I'm familiar with most kids that hang out with ours). The atmosphere was usually friendly. I introduced myself and spoke to the kid and confessed

I didn't remember seeing him around campus before and he said in a polite southern accent, "Ma'am my school and home was destroyed in Katrina and the Headmaster took in a few us here" (for the sake of political correctness "headmasters" are now called "the head of school"). We chatted it up for a few minutes and I told him to have his mom contact me if there was anything she wanted/needed me to do. He mentioned how nice and welcoming everyone had been to him. I excused myself and went to the bathroom and cried. Here this kid had lost everything (except his parents) yet he was good spirited and polite. This was the epitome of appreciation. It was also gracious of the Brooks school to house and educate Katrina victims.

We don't have to let total strangers move into our homes, I don't' necessarily see any wisdom in that. We can offer to put them up in a motel or other acceptable place that isn't too expensive even if we need to make a financial sacrifice in order to make it happen.

The place of worship I attended when our sons were ten and nine solicited members to host kids from the African Children's Choir. My husband and I opened our home to three kids and one adult for about a week. It was one of the best experiences of my life! The children were well-mannered boys and set perfect examples for our children, who generically tried to mimic them. The kids we were assigned were from Uganda and appreciated every little thing I did for them. They called me "Aunty" and would ask to be excused before leaving the table. They'd offered to help cook and wash dishes, which was something I definitely was not used to hearing! The weather was beautiful outside but they preferred to stay inside and play chess or other board games. Unbelievable! They flipped when they learned we had the *Disney's Lion King* movie on DVD and pleaded with me to let them see it. I told them it was okay with me if it was okay with their chaperone, which it was so I popped them some popcorn and served juice and they sat quietly from start to finish gazing at the animated characters that I imagine came to life in their minds.

Viewing the movie was the gateway for them to ask to see more movies but they didn't. They thanked me profusely and offered to help with housework. In retrospect, I wished I hadn't cleaned up before they arrived because they could have been my house cleaning helpers. I'm just kidding! There's no way I would have turned their stay into manual labor. Besides, they had a show to perform and rehearsal schedules to keep. They were extremely professional too! The audience was amazed and gave them standing ovations.

All I did was open up my home and feed them. The organization that coordinated the visit of the African Children's Choir were extremely organized and professional. Plus, a couple of my neighbors gave me money for groceries. My husband and I did not come one cent out of our pockets we only provided rooms for them to sleep and transportation.

The point is that giving back comes in many forms. And, you'd be surprised by how good it feels to give. Giving generously and from the heart can also help reverse the aging process as well as have the potential to relieve stress because if you're doing acts of giving chances are you're not thinking about personal problems. You open yourself up to experience what it feels like to help others – especially those in need. You can simultaneously erase age-deterrent wrinkles while being an asset to another cause.

There are so many commitments one can perform at any adult age. Minors can also partake in helping others with the permission of their parents. Matter of fact, if people start in their youth it wouldn't be something foreign to them by the time they become grownups. And when they become adults hopefully it would be a habitual way of life to be givers to other people and positive causes.

In case you're wondering the aforementioned relates to *This Side of Forty* because we are encouraged to consider broadening our scope to include going further in human compassion. It doesn't matter if we are under or over forty. We can start helping from our current position. I'm not recommending that you go outside your comfort zone by doing something you simply don't know how to do. I'm no medical doctor and if someone asked me to go to a third world country to treat patients I'd be at a total loss. On the other hand, I could go to a third world country to help feed starving kids and people in general. Our agency is our service by helping others.

Maybe we could read to sick children in hospitals right here in America or wherever you may live. Maybe to orphans in orphanages. We can find a way to benefit others without spending money such as donate our time. I defy anyone to reach out to others and not change a life. You may not instantly receive a personal benefit and that's okay. Maybe you're setting yourself up to receive some fantastic thing that's currently stuck in the ethers because you're too stingy to release your money, service, or time?

Maybe you don't feel the need to help others because no one was around to help you when you were struggling and if this is the case why would you not want to help others? You know how it felt to struggle so why would you not want to help ease that pain for someone else? Could it be that you're too self-centered? Get a clue; you might be sabotaging yourself if you're selfish or too self-centered to help others in need? Could it be that you choose not to help others because no one helped you during your time of need? Or is it possible that in the flow of life's busyness it never actually occurred to you to reach out and help others? If this is the case, moving forward, please consider what method to choose to help others who are not as fortunate as you.

Are you the type to help others and then brag about it? Really? You don't have to make a big deal over doing good deeds for others. People see you and know about your deeds; and even if people don't recognize it the universe does so you don't have to toot your own horn for goodness sakes.

There are those that give for the sole purpose of making themselves appear superior. We can dispute their motives but at least they gave…for whatever reason. Somewhere inside they possess generosity otherwise no matter how it seems they would keep their donations to themselves if they were stingy. My hope for this crew is they become givers from the hearts without possessing questionable motives, which could actually somehow help them when their giving becomes pure.

Giving back can also be accomplished in day-to-day routines such as the work place. Company higher ups such as presidents, vice presidents, managers, mid-managers, supervisors and all that have leadership positions should consider how they affect the people they lead and know it's a reflection of themselves. Strong leadership is not obnoxious. Successful leaders should know how to tap into the strengths of their subordinates, or if you prefer, their support staff. Successful leaders also know how to lead without being egocentric. The egocentric leader barks out orders and control atmospheres that are thick enough to be cut with a butter knife. On the other hand, the mature non-egocentric leader knows how to meet goals without evoking fear or threats to employees. The mature leader understands that more company goals are met, and perhaps exceeded, because when employees are relaxed they are inspired to be more productive as they work.

Another point worthy of consideration is that if we continue in unprofitable habits we will continue to yield unprofitable results. We must consider that for things to change we must first absolutely make up our minds to steer our mindsets towards the "I can" accomplish whatever it is I desire to accomplish; then put this newfound mindset into motion. How to put mindsets into motion? If you can read, you have every tool at your disposal; but if you cannot read you have access to free education in America and can be taught how to read at any age.

If you already know how to read practically all information about everything is accessible through the world-wide-web. And you don't have to own a computer to access the Internet. You can obtain a library card and use public computers for free to search the Internet. Or you can read and research the traditional way by reading reference and how-to books in order to obtain leads that steer you in the direction of obtaining your goals. You can essentially educate yourself on how to become better at the skill or talent that brings you joy; or you can connect with others that are doing what you desire and learn from them.

If you don't have the inclination to learn how to read, you still have the ability to develop whatever skill you have and have the option of entrusting others around you that are business savvy to help connect you with companies that can catapult your skill and hopefully turn it into profit.

I used to tutor a kid that had a serious learning disability and required special learning tools. This kid was a slow learner and I felt helpless because most tutors that came in contact with him quickly grew weary and impatient, which did not help. I discovered that he was a brilliant artist and expressed to his mother, who also seem frustrated about his lack of academic focus, that his talent as an artist could someday make him wealthy. I took the liberty of telling her to allow him to flourish as an artist because it was truly his strongest gift that I observed. He drew pictures that were loaded with untraced detail; and one doesn't have to be a professional curator to see how truly talented that little boy was. Looking back, I wished I would have kept at least one of his pictures and asked him to autograph it for me.

It is my belief that college isn't for everyone. I didn't appreciate college until after I was married with children. Of course, I don't recommend going in the opposite path by postponing college for too long because it could especially be more challenging for people like me who struggle to retain information. College carries a lot of weight to most employers because it states that an individual was structured and focused enough to receive a liberal education that helps them become more well-rounded. People that carry the same discipline from academia into the workforce will also most likely have success in their careers. Those that believe there aren't enough jobs available must find a way to create their own opportunities.

We mustn't discount trade schools and other programs that might be a better match for our skills. There are thousands of successful people that never went to college. Of these thousands, many may have taken a course or two here or there in order to become better at what they're already doing for their livelihoods; yet the main thing they understand is the significance of movement and an above average work ethic. I've personally never seen or met a broke person that is motivated, willing to make sacrifices and has outstanding work ethic. I'm sure it might exist and you have my permission to challenge me on this point. Every motivated person I've ever met always either have careers or some type of legal hustle where they are generating an income. What I know with certainty is that nothing gets accomplished by sitting still; neither does anything gets accomplished by expecting it to come easily!

*This Side of Forty* seeks to pour into the life of the entire populace with great encouragement regardless of age. *TSOF* wants you to embrace your current age, don't believe negative flimflam and realize it's never too late for you to become a better you. Look at the glass as being half-full. Look at your age and life through hopeful lens. If you don't like your current age, consider how temporary it is because it only lasts one year. Be determined to enjoy your life at every age because you only have one life to live (no pun intended).

Many may have cheated life by escaping something catastrophic; and if this is you, what have you done for yourself lately? What have you done for someone else lately? Did you decide to change your life for the better after your close encounter with the gloom you narrowly escaped? If you're one of those rare persons that was in a life-threatening situation and cheated death, take time to be more fabulous, positive and of course lend a helping hand to others in need.

Hopefully all will come to realize that we have what it takes within us to better our lives and I believe it starts with making wise choices as well as goal setting. We can determine within ourselves to not let another day pass being confined to whatever we believe is holding us back. This, my friends, will be the beginning of something fantastic to happen for us whether we are on this side or that side of forty! Love y'all!!! 😊.

The following poem created by me was inspired by my two sons who to this day I believe are walking miracles. I'm sharing it with those who are affected by medical challenges and want you to know that hope truly does spring eternal:

# My Heart's Desire

When they said I'd never get pregnant
Having a baby became most urgent.
You know, I've always been kind of stubborn
Inner temper as hot as an oven.
Now I tell myself not to panic
Because this isn't the worst thing on the planet.
After all God said be 'fruitful and multiply'
And just this once I wanted to comply.

I took the drugs I took the tests
Unfavorable results left me unable to rest.

Surprisingly one day out of the blue
My wildest dream had finally come true.
I called my mother to tell her the story
She was happy for me, in all of my glory.

I went to the doctor for my next check-up
Dreading every minute of my heels in the stirrups.
I knew by the doctor's facial expression

*That something was wrong with this conception.*
*The fetus was weak and had to be taken*
*My husband and mother, both were quite shaken.*

*I spoke to the devil and called him a liar*
*Because God already told me, I'd get my heart's desire.*

*Eleven months later I got pregnant and gave birth*
*To our new baby boy, born on May twenty-first.*
*He was healthy and strong and brought us much joy*
*Then eleven months from that came another baby boy!*

*People call my babies "Irish twins" with wavy hair*
*This I don't mind because I now have a pair.*

*Medical pros can predict you might die*
*But as for me I'm gonna listen, to the One from on High!*

*- Minister Cathy Glen*

# About the Author

*C*athy Glen earned her bachelor's degree in liberal arts from Columbia College in Chicago before going on to receive her master's degree in biblical studies at Moody Theological Seminary, also in Chicago. In 2001 she was awarded with the Editor's Choice Award for Outstanding Achievement in Poetry from the International Library of Poetry. Cathy and her husband, Timothy, raised their two sons, one nephew and live in Chicago.

Questions? Please contact me at: ThisSideofForty@gmail.com for constructive questions and feedback.

Printed in the United States
By Bookmasters